The BEGINNER'S GUIDE *to* BIRDING

The BEGINNER'S GUIDE *to*
BIRDING

*The Easiest Way
for Anyone to Explore
the Incredible World of Birds*

NATE SWICK

editor of the ABA Blog and
writer for 10,000 Birds

PAGE STREET
PUBLISHING CO.

PAGE STREET
PUBLISHING CO.

*To Danielle, without whom none of this
would have been possible*

CONTENTS

FOREWORD

A mad, magical passion for watching birds in their element motivates millions of Americans every day to explore the highways, byways, and secret trails of our wild world. You may very soon find yourself doing the same. And yet, birding culture feels surprisingly close; everyone seems to recognize everyone else's name. This is to say that, if you explore nature in North Carolina or enjoy reading about birding online, you may already know Nate Swick, or at least feel like you know him.

Online is where I first met Nate, through his blog The Drinking Bird, the title of which probably doesn't mean what you think it means. What struck me about Nate wasn't just his obvious passion for birding; most avian enthusiasts are equally fervent. Nate stood out through the clarity and cleverness of his writing. He understood, even at his relatively young age, so much about birds, birding, and nature. But, more important, he wanted to share those insights so that others understood as well.

For a long time, I thought that combination of birding and writing acumen defined Nate's genius and certainly explained why, from our initial meeting, I sought him out to collaborate on every crazy idea I had. In 2008, when the Nature Blog Network, serving thousands of nature bloggers around the world, needed a community coordinator, Nate was the guy. In 2010, when we transitioned 10,000 Birds to a group blog, Nate was the guy. In 2012, when we resurrected the popular blog carnival I and the Bird, Nate was the guy. Whenever a project demanded a brilliant communicator who understood how to connect and educate this naturalist community we were both a part of, Nate was always the guy.

And I wasn't the only collaborator clamoring to work with Nate. When the revitalized American Birding Association, in the midst of a series of brilliant moves, decided to get serious about connecting with its community, Jeff Gordon brought Nate on board to manage the ABA blog. Since then, Nate has acquired more responsibilities and titles at the ABA, which only makes sense for someone as capable, talented, and effective as Nate is at this whole "writing about birding" thing, as you are about to find out.

This book, this essential guide to getting started on what may be the most satisfying hobby you've ever known, offers the ideal gateway to birding. Of course you'll learn where and how and with whom to best enjoy watching birds. Most important, though, you'll understand why you really should try birding, knowing that once you do, you may be hooked!

Nate has always been a linchpin, the kind of communicator and coordinator every community needs to thrive. Perhaps this is because when you are raised as a wild rambler by a science teacher dad and find yourself lighting that spark of passion for nature in your own children, birding represents more than just a culture or community: It becomes a family affair. Over the years, Nate has introduced more and more grateful individuals to this larger community, this vast family of bird watchers and nature lovers.

With this book you hold in your fortunate hands, he is connecting you too. Welcome!

—*Mike Bergin, Founder of 10,000 Birds and the Nature Blog Network*

Chapter 1

WHY BIRDS?

Talk to any birder or bird-watcher, and the answer to that question might be different for every individual. It can't be as simple as the fact that birds can fly, can it? Or their irrefutable link to dinosaurs? Or the subconscious lure of the cartoon characters adorning the TV shows and breakfast cereal boxes of our childhood? Whatever the draw, there's something to birds that has always fascinated people. It doesn't hurt that birds are truly everywhere present in our lives, in ways that we often take for granted. That is, until we decide to become clued-in to them.

From my own perspective, the most remarkable thing for a person new to bird-watching is the realization that incredible things are occurring all around, all the time. And until you know what to look for, you can be completely unaware of it all. The blackbirds in your yard in the spring are not the same ones in your yard in the winter. The robin at the park in New York might have been in Florida a day ago. The sandpipers chasing the waves at the beach in the summer might spend their winters dodging your vacationing *doppelganger* in Brazil. And every night in spring and fall, literally millions of birds are moving above your head, their direction depending on the season, and their image more or less invisible unless you were to train binoculars at the moon and watch the tiny specks passing in front of its face.

Bird-watching is a quest for the remarkable, the beautiful, the incredible. It's the closest thing many of us can get to becoming Sherlock Holmes or Indiana Jones for a few hours. Average birders have the ability to make discoveries, to contribute to science, to find meaning in a national park or a local landfill (though you may want to hold off a bit on that second one). You'll meet amazing people whose generosity of spirit and eagerness to spread the gospel of birding will consistently amaze you. Birding can take you to far-flung places, to parts of the world you'd never think of visiting if not for the birds there. Or it can make you more aware of the fascinating world in your own backyard. The birding world is big. There's a place for everybody in it.

At the very basic level, the one thing that makes birders different from non-birders is simply the ability to notice more. Fortunately, this isn't difficult to accomplish; it only requires a minor change of perspective, and this is possible no matter where you might live.

ACTIVITY 1:
LOOKING LIKE A BIRDER

Every potential hobby has tools of the trade, and birding is no different. A birder will need a field guide or two, binoculars, a notebook, sketchpad, and a camera. But for the time being, none of that is really necessary. I'm not asking you to deck yourself out in a khaki vest and wide-brimmed hat just yet. What I mean by looking like a birder is learning to see like a birder. Use your senses to be aware of the natural activity surrounding you. Think about what motivates birds, and use that to focus your attention.

Like so many humans, birds are primarily motivated by two things, eating and breeding. They are easiest to discover when they're focusing on either of these things. Birds looking to eat go to places where they can find food. Birds looking to breed sing loudly and conspicuously in search of mates. Good places to bird-watch are places where they're doing both, but don't think that these need to be special places; they can be as simple as the bird feeder in your yard or a small pond in your neighborhood.

Here's how to get started:

1. Head outside and start listening for something, anything, that sounds "birdy," and track it down. Birds are most often heard before they're seen, so this is a good way to start. Try to be aware of the different types of sounds that you hear. The different sounds can be broken down into two broadly defined groups: songs and calls, and these sounds mean different things. Songs are often fluid and complex, but calls are short, simple, and inconspicuous.

2. Birds sing to attract mates or to designate a territory. They call to keep in contact with others of their own or other species. A singing bird will likely stay in the same place for an extended period of time, belting out a song. A calling bird may be moving along, out of sight, actively feeding or even flying over. Try to recognize what you are hearing, and use that knowledge to know where to look to see your quarry.

3. Look for places where food might be found. This can be a fruiting berry bush, a patch of mud attracting flies, or a flowering tree with buzzing insects. Birds will often be in these places, but the specific places where birds tend to congregate will change based on the time of year and what kind of birds they are. This will be covered in greater detail in Chapter 8.

4. Once you find an area with some bird activity, stop and attempt to get a good look at one or more of the birds you see. Identifying it is less important now. It's better to think about what it's doing, and how it's moving. Is it flitting around in the leaves? Is it creeping up or down a tree trunk? Does it flit its wings or bob its tail? Note its colors and patterns in broad strokes, and don't get too hung up on specifics just yet. Shape, color, and behavior are the important things to think about, once you want to begin identifying the birds you see. That's how you'll be able to tell a woodpecker (tree-trunk creeper, black-and-white pattern) from a kinglet (branch-tips, wing-flitter, small, plain) a sparrow (ground-hugging, streaky, thick bill) or a hawk (large, slow-movements, hooked bill).

(continued on page 18)

Birds like warblers have a long, narrow beak for probing for insects in leaves and flowers.

A short, conical beak is found on birds like sparrows and finches that feed primarily on seeds.

A duck's bill is long and broad for filter feeding small organisms in the water.

A jay's beak is like a Swiss army knife, thick and sturdy for a generalist diet.

Short, hooked beaks for tearing meat can be found on all raptor families.

Noticing the shape of a bird's beak can give you clues as to what it does and where you can find it.

Short "arms" and long hands on a bird like this swallow, allow for quick, maneuverable flight perfect for catching flying insects.

The long, broad wings of an eagle allow it to soar effortlessly as it searches for food on land or in the water.

Duck wings are relatively short compared to their heavy bodies, but perfect for fast, straight-line flight.

Gull wings are broad and pointed, great for maneuvering and soaring in changing coastal wind conditions.

Most perching birds have broad, rounded wings, splitting the difference between speed and loft for efficient movement.

The shape of a bird's wings can tell you a lot about how a species lives and how you can find it.

5. Most birds in urban or suburban areas are pretty familiar with the actions of humans, so long as those humans are paying them no mind. Once you focus on the birds around you, they'll notice, and start acting a little warier. Slow, sidelong movements are better than walking directly up to them. Obscure your movements with trees and brush. You don't need to stalk or anything, but be conscious of how the birds are perceiving you. If they look alert—stretched out and quiet, stop for a bit and let them get adjusted before you move forward again.

The ability to enjoy and appreciate wild birds is a skill you can apply to any situation, wherever you are in the world. Wherever you go, there will be new birds, new birders, and new places to explore. For many bird-watchers, birding is an excuse to get outdoors, to see new things, or to challenge themselves. Being aware of the birds around you is like knowing a secret, one that will enrich your life in ways you may never have imagined.

Opening your eyes and beginning to pay attention to what is happening around you is the first step. Welcome. Now you're a birder.

Chapter 2

YOUR FIELD GUIDE TO FIELD GUIDES

The point at which you cross over from being a person who notices birds to being an "official" birder is the point at which you begin to try to identify the birds you see.

There are nearly a thousand species of birds on the official list for the United States and Canada, and trying to get your head around all those can seem to be a daunting task. But the truth of the matter is that, depending on where you live, ninety percent of the birds you see are going to be from a few dozen common species. Once you expend that little effort it takes to get a handle on those species, you'll have a good foundation on which to build your skill.

Knowing the basics is important for a few other reasons too. Identifying birds is an exercise in comparisons, and it's important to have a baseline so you have something to compare to. Saying a bird is small or red or brown is not as useful for identification as saying it's smaller than an American Robin or brighter red than a Summer Tanager. When birders talk to each other about identifying birds, this is the language they use, so getting familiar with it is a good idea. But how should you begin to learn those starter birds to which everything is compared? Get yourself a field guide.

FIELD GUIDES 101

A good field guide is the first piece of birding-specific equipment you'll want to get, and arguably the most important. Most bookstores have entire shelves devoted to field guides to North American birds. And with new titles coming out seemingly every year—every one trying to reinvent the wheel—it can seem overwhelming. Ultimately, though, this book diversity is a good thing for the birder. With so many options covering what is essentially the same information, an interested birder is more likely to find a guide that best speaks to him. Just about every title has its proponents and detractors, and it's a good idea to head to your local bookstore or bird supply store to flip through many of them to find the one you like best.

FIELD GUIDES WORTH CONSIDERING

1. ***The Sibley Guide to Birds:*** To many birders, this is the gold standard. Sibley's illustrations are true to life and show birds in a variety of angles and plumages. Sibley doesn't focus on details, putting a premium on patterns rather than individual feathers. The "big Sibley," around $40, features both eastern and western birds. You can get smaller guides limited to East or West for $20.

2. ***National Geographic Field Guide to Birds of North America:*** This is another favorite. Jon Dunn and Jonathan Alderford have managed to fit all the birds of the continental United States and Canada into a smaller package than the big Sibley. Multiple illustrators make for a more uneven style, but that's a minor point. This is the most complete guide out there. $30.

3. ***Peterson Field Guide to Birds of North America:*** Roger Tory Peterson is the father of American birding, and his field guide is still a favorite for many. I'm not as high on it as on the previous two, but many birders still swear by it. $27.

4. ***Kaufman Field Guide to Birds of North America:*** Kenn Kaufman is one of North America's finest field birders, and his guide is excellent for distilling the field marks and behaviors of birds into memorable phrases. This guide uses photos that have been "enhanced" to bring out important field marks, which some like but others find too strange. Definitely one of the better photo guides, however. $20.

5. ***ABA Field Guides:*** The new series of American Birding Association guides to individual states is a good bet for those overwhelmed by the options of a continent-wide guide. These books feature only the birds likely to be seen in a certain state, which is great if you live in one of those states. Currently, guides to New Jersey, Colorado, and Florida have been released, with New York, Pennsylvania, Minnesota, Arizona, California, Texas, North Carolina, and others in production. $25 each.

Descriptions often include habitat, notable behaviors, and transcribed vocalizations.

Similar species are grouped together for easy comparison.

Maps color-coded to season.

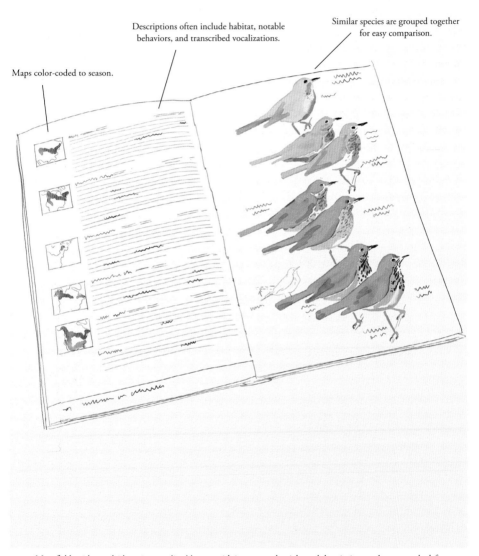

Most field guides are laid out in a predictable way, with images on the right and descriptions and maps on the left.

A field guide is kind of an odd combination of science textbook and practical manual, but for the most part, the layout is pretty standard. Open to any random page and you're likely to see the right side devoted to illustrations or photographs of birds with important field marks noted or labeled and the left side offering relevant information, usually consisting of a map showing where a bird is present in different seasons and a short paragraph about important things to look for when identifying it like behavior or common vocalizations.

With limited space available, authors often use shorthand and jargon. Most guides include an extensive foreword section explaining how to use the book and some of the more confusing aspects, like bird-part terminology or whatever sort of gibberish the author has chosen to illustrate what bird vocalizations sound like. It's easy to overlook this part of a field guide, and most people will skip over it to get to the flashy pictures, but it often contains really useful information. Reading this part of the book often feels like eating your Brussels sprouts or flossing your teeth, but at the risk of sounding too much like your mom, it's good for you. You may not be at the point where you need or want to know the difference between tertials and coverts—heck, it's fine if you never get there—but it's good to know that both of those are parts of the wing. Knowing how to identify birds is about knowing what and where to look for things. Some of those things can be incredibly specific, so the more you know about where to look, the better off you'll be as your skills improve.

PHOTO VS. ILLUSTRATION: THE GREAT DEBATE

Some field guides use photos. Some use illustrations, either by one artist or many. The argument over which is better has been raging ever since cameras became advanced enough and ubiquitous enough to take high-quality photos of birds.

Some birders swear by illustrations because only an artist can capture the ideal representation of a given species or paint it in such a way as to emphasize characteristics that help identification and de-emphasize those that confuse.

Each individual bird is unique in the same way that each human being is, and a photo of one may not look like a photo of another of the same species. Photos are confusing, some say. But a photo can show a bird as it appears in the field, which is an obvious advantage because birds are living things that don't always perch the way they do in illustrated field guides—in perfect profile and with all relevant field marks observable—and a good picture taken by one photographer looks a lot like a good picture by another photographer. Photos also offer a continuity that isn't always available in books with several different illustrators, where one artist's style can make a bird look very different from the same species drawn by another artist.

The argument rages, and likely will never be settled because each point in favor of photos or illustrations has some truth to it. It ultimately comes down to the preference of the birder but, if you become serious at all about birds, you'll probably end up with at least one of each anyway.

As for me, I reach for a guide with illustrations first, because I prefer the standardized positions. But like many birders, I have many field guides to choose from.

The Structure of the Field Guide

Most field guides put birds in phylogenetic order, which is a scientific way of saying that birds closely related to each other evolutionarily are going to be grouped together in the book. Most of the time this makes sense. Gulls and terns, for instance, are both beach birds, are closely related, and are near each other in pretty much every field guide. Piece of cake, right?

But there are some relationships that are counterintuitive. Hawks and falcons are both daytime raptors, and birders often see them in the same places doing similar things. Recent research looking deep into their genes, however, shows they're not very closely related at all. So in most newer field guides, you'll find the hawks grouped with the eagles, and the falcons near the parrots. Parrots, it turns out, are falcons' nearest relatives—think about that next time you square off with a pet cockatiel. Arguments have been made by many field guide authors that the science of birds and the study of birds as a hobby are sort of at odds here. If you want to identify a soaring hawky-falcon raptor thing, it's nice to have all those birds right next to each other in the guide for comparison. So some guides may use a modified order, mostly phylogenetic, but with an eye toward easy usage for novices.

ACTIVITY 2:
BUYING AND USING A FIELD GUIDE

1. **Travel to your local bookstore or bird supply store and flip through the available guides.** You can try to get an idea of what are popular choices by talking to other birders or the clerks at the stores. For obvious reasons, a bird supply store will probably have more insight. Pick three or so field guides to peruse. Make sure you have included at least one with illustrations and one with photos. Choose a common species you are familiar with, and look at that bird in all three field guides. Focus on things you know about the bird, and determine which guide or guides have the best representation of the bird you're familiar with.

2. **Look at supplementary information.** Maps and descriptions are every bit as important as the images. Maps, for instance, will be color-coordinated with one color representing where the bird is in summer, another where the bird is in winter, and so forth. There's no standard, though, so make sure the representation is intuitive to you. Blue for summer and green for winter doesn't make a lot of sense, but some field guides will go this way. Descriptions of bird behavior and appearance are also important. Every field guide author writes these things a little differently, and some are more skilled than others. You'll certainly want to go with the guide in which the information makes the most sense to you. Perhaps one uses too much jargon or the vocalizations are confusing. Maybe one writes in a way that is particularly memorable to you. Don't be afraid to be discerning.

3. **Look at regional guides.** Maybe the big guide that covers the entire continent is too much for you. Most guides break the continent down into two sections, east and west, and limit the birds inside to the birds you are most likely to see in those regions. This might be a good place to start to avoid overwhelming yourself. You may also see a number of state/province–specific guides. These are not always as useful, though a new series by the ABA, mentioned earlier in this chapter, is certainly worth checking out if your home state/province is covered.

4. **Buy the guide you like the most.** It's the one you're most likely to use.

ONCE YOU GET IT HOME

Put your field guide in a prominent place. If you want to learn birds, you have to do your homework. Fortunately, this homework can be fun. Put your field guide in a place where you'll see it. When you have some free time or down time, pick it up and page through it. Not only will you begin to get a feel for the order of the birds in your guide, you'll be amping yourself up for your next birding experience by finding birds you want to see and learning what to look for *before* you see them.

Learn how to use the maps. Too often birders will ignore the maps in favor of the images of the birds, but those maps are as important to figuring out what you're seeing as the pictures of the actual bird. They tell you whether you should expect to see a bird near your home and, if so, when you're going to see it. For instance, Carolina and Black-Capped Chickadees are extremely similar in appearance, but there is only a narrow band where they are going to overlap. If you live in the South and you think you're seeing a Black-Capped Chickadee, check that map again! Birds are pretty predictable. They mostly return to the same places year after year. Knowing when and where you won't see them is important too, because it narrows down those 900-plus choices to something more manageable.

Lastly, don't carry your field guide in the field. I know, counterintuitive, right? But if you do your homework, you'll be free in the field to look at birds rather than at your book. I guarantee that you'll see more.

PUTTING THE GUIDE TO WORK

One of the most important things you can do with your field guide is to get comfortable with how the birds are ordered. The hawks are in one section, the ducks in another, perching birds take up the back half. Don't be afraid to use sticky notes to create tabs for quick reference. Some field guides already do this by assigning colors to the groups or scalloped thumb tabs to help you find families.

Head back out in your neighborhood, or watch your feeder for a while, armed with this new knowledge, and try to find representatives of as many groups as you can and identify at least one from each group.

1. **Ducks**–Usually toward the beginning of your guide. They can be found on any body of water. Determine by behavior whether they're dabbling ducks or diving ducks, and turn to the right section accordingly. Males are usually brightly colored and patterned, and easier to identify early on.

2. **Hawks**–In the front half of the guide. Common groups include Buteos with broad wings and short tails and Accipiters with shorter wings and long tails. Often soaring above or hiding near a feeding station, looking to strike.

3. **Woodpeckers**–Toward the end of the first half of most guides. Usually patterned black and white, and vertically oriented on tree trunks and branches. Many species are fans of acorns in fall and winter and can be found around oak trees.

4. **Warblers**–Middle-back of your guide. Most species are seasonally abundant, but in winter Yellow-Rumped Warblers are common continent-wide in roaming flocks, along with chickadees.

5. **Sparrows**–Toward the end of your guide. Mostly streaky, brown or gray, and commonly on the ground or near tall grasses and shrubs. Listen for scratching sounds among fallen leaves to find them feeding under bushes.

Chapter 3

BINOCULARIA

There's no tool that is more associated with birders than a pair of binoculars slung around the neck. And, while a field guide might be a more useful possession particularly early on, it's the binoculars that make the birder.

All told, binoculars are a pretty simple tool: Two metal tubes with a few lenses inside that make faraway things look closer. But as you'll quickly realize, those tubes and those lenses are not all made the same. There are a wide variety of styles, sizes, and prices that you'll want to consider before making a purchase. And while the old pair kicking around in the back of the closet will get you out the door and into the field, at a certain point, you'll probably want something of a little more quality if you're going to be interested in this birding thing. A good pair of binoculars can make the difference between a great day exploring the birds around you and a frustrating day fighting the limitations of your glass. Fortunately, you don't have to spend a ton of money on something that won't frustrate you (though you certainly can), and this chapter intends to give you the rundown on what to look for.

Before diving in, a couple bits of terminology. The part of the binoculars you look into is called the eyepiece. The lens at the other end is the objective lens. Most binoculars have a focus knob somewhere in the middle that you can adjust to sharpen the image. And that's pretty much it.

They are remarkably analog pieces of equipment in a world, and a hobby, that has seen a lot of electronic influence. And while computers have improved the manufacturing process (and the resulting quality and value), the binoculars themselves are essentially the same device people have used for hundreds of years. That's pretty amazing.

PORRO PRISM VS. ROOF PRISM STYLES

Binoculars come in two styles, porro prism and roof prism. In non-jargon terms, you can think of them as angled and straight. For a very long time, porro (angled) prism was the standard because it was too expensive to mass-produce roof (straight-barreled) prism binoculars. Now you can get both, but roofs predominate, particularly at the high end.

With two pairs of binoculars, one of each type at the same price, the porro prisms are usually going to have the better optical quality. This is because they have fewer lenses to cause distortion. But roof-prism binoculars have advantages too. They're usually lighter, more comfortable to hold and—let's be honest here—they look cooler. Plus, you'll have more options, whatever you're looking to spend.

In roof prism binoculars, the light goes straight through the barrel into your eye.

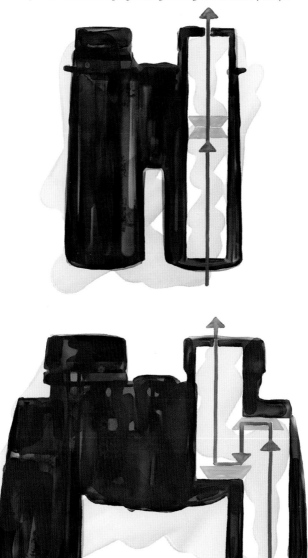

Porro prism binoculars have offset lenses, so the light banks through the barrel. They tend to be less expensive, but are heavier and often lack waterproofing.

What do those numbers mean?

You'll notice that binoculars are labeled using two numbers: *7 x 32* or *10 x 50*, etc. The first number refers to the magnification power. If your eyes see at 1x power, a *7x* binocular will help you see 7 times closer, a *10x* will make it 10 times closer and so on. You might think that a higher magnification is automatically better, but there are other aspects to consider. Higher magnification usually requires more light, so the image will be a bit darker the higher up you go. And while the object looks bigger at higher magnification, it also means that any tremor or bump will be bigger too. Holding the binoculars steady becomes more difficult the more powerful the lenses are.

Also, a higher magnification means a narrower field of view. Field of view is the width of the image you see through the binoculars—think of it as the binoculars' peripheral vision. Field of view is more important for eyeglass-wearers than anyone else, and while it's something to be aware of, it's not something that birders need to put too much weight onto when considering a pair of binoculars.

The second number is the diameter, in millimeters, of the objective lens. Remember, this is the end you point at what you want to see. A larger objective lets in more light (which is why high-magnification binoculars usually have a big objective lens) but it's also heavier. A larger piece of glass is usually more costly to manufacture, meaning a more expensive binocular.

The most popular arrangements for birders are any combination of *7x* or *8x* magnification with a *32mm* or *42mm* lens. These offer the best magnification to weight/price/quality.

Cost vs. Value

If you're looking to purchase some binoculars, one of the first things you'll notice is how expensive some of them are. It's true, some of the finest binoculars in the world can cost upward of $2,500, and the price seemingly increases every year with every new model. Understandably, this can put some people off; but in recent years, manufacturers have made great strides in making affordable, quality binoculars. In fact, there are binoculars in the $300-to-$500 range these days that are as good or better than those that cost over $1,000 a decade ago. And $300 is about where you begin to find binoculars that are well-built enough to handle "field conditions," which can include harsh weather, near-constant handling, and most important, reckless tosses into the car at the end of the day. At that price point, you likely won't be fidgeting or complaining about your binoculars while you're out looking at birds. There's nothing worse than equipment letting you down when you need it, as anyone attempting a home project on the cheap can attest to.

The difference between a $500 pair and one that costs $2,500 is both subtle and stark. The more expensive binoculars tend to be assembled by hand rather than machine, and the glass used will usually have fewer flaws, along with high-quality coatings (which enhance contrast and improve low-light images, among other things). Eighty-five percent of the time, you might not be able to tell the difference if you looked through both of them, but for some birders, that fifteen percent in low-light or difficult conditions matters. It's a decision for the individual birder to make.

The rule of thumb is to buy the best-quality binoculars you can afford at the time. This certainly means different things to different people, but I've never heard anyone complain about purchasing a slightly more expensive binocular than they intended. If you enjoy birding, it's worth it to make a purchase that reflects the level of enjoyment you get out of it.

TRY THEM OUT

As with field guides, when purchasing binoculars, it's a good idea to head to a birding supply store or a sporting goods store with a good selection and try them out. Even seemingly similar binoculars can feel different in the hand.

Try to read signs from across the room, and pay attention to edges of the field of view. Hold the binoculars in your hand, and put the strap around your neck. Are they heavy around your neck? Does any part of the binocular rub your hands in an uncomfortable way? Would you be able to pick them up and put them down dozens of times in a morning? If you do not wear glasses, are the eyecups comfortable? Can you adjust them to the proper width? These are all questions to consider.

Every birder seems to have an opinion or recommendation for a great pair of binoculars. At mid-range, brands like Nikon, Vortex, and Eagle Optics offer great value for the money. Eagle Optics, based in Wisconsin, is a mostly online retailer, so you can't try out the binoculars before you buy. Their warranty is exceptional, however, and they will replace a pair of binoculars if you don't like them.

If money is no object, you cannot go wrong with the big European brands, Leica, Zeiss, and Swarovski.

ACTIVITY 3:
YOU'VE GOT YOUR BINOCULARS. NOW WHAT?

Let's use them!

Like most things, using binoculars naturally requires a bit of practice. Before you head out into the field, it's a good idea to get comfortable with your new toy.

Here are some tips:

1. Find an immobile object in your backyard or in your house. Without moving your eyes from that object, raise the binoculars to your eyes. (If you look down as you raise your binoculars, you'll probably lose the object, because your peripheral vision is much reduced through binoculars.)

2. Find the focus knob, and turn it until the object is tack sharp. Practice this until you can do it without thinking.

3. Once you've mastered that, head outside and practice on moving objects. You don't need to look just at birds; anything that is moving around works. Airplanes, squirrels, pets, your own children. (I'd avoid using them on other people's kids. The interactions can be awkward....)

4. Remember to keep your eyes on the object as you lift the binoculars to your eyes.

5. If the object is moving, follow it with the binoculars. You may need to adjust focus as it moves because the depth of field is much narrower through binoculars. Being able to do this naturally takes time and practice. But once you're pretty comfortable, you are ready to go!

With your right eye closed, focus on an object in the middle distance until it is tack sharp.

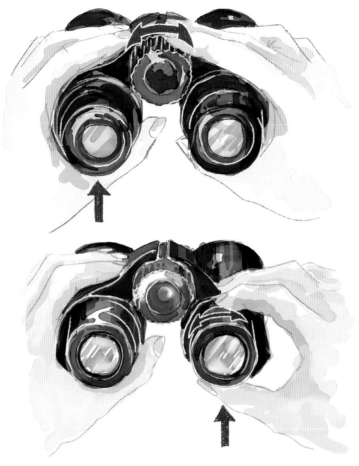

Now close your left eye and turn the diopter until the object is sharp again. Adjusting the dopter correctly is critical to getting the most out of your bins.

One last thing to consider: Just as you're right- or left-handed, you can be right- or left-eyed. Even with corrective lenses, your eyes are likely different strengths. As with everything else, this difference is magnified when using binoculars. Fortunately, you can adjust for it.

On every pair of binoculars, there is an adjustment knob called a diopter. It's usually a zero (0) with a plus symbol (+) to one side and a minus (-) on the other. It can either be on one of the eyepieces or near the focus knob, depending on the make and model of your binoculars. This device is intended to correct for the differences between your eyes, and too few birders know how to use it properly.

Adjusting the diopter:

1. Place the diopter at zero. Using a lens cover (in a pinch you can close your eye), cover the objective lens of the barrel that the diopter is on (usually the right).

2. Find an object in the middle distance, and use the main focus knob to get the image as sharp as you can.

3. Move the lens cover to the other barrel (or close your other eye), and look at the same object.

4. Keeping the focus knob exactly where it is, adjust the diopter toward the + or – until the image is as sharp as you can get it.

5. When you look at the image now, it should be sharp, and you should feel no eyestrain.

Now that you've got your tools, let's get to the fun stuff.

Let's go birding!

Chapter 4

HOW TO ID
WHAT YOU SEE

Now that you've got your field guide, you've probably begun to flip through it and are more aware than ever of the incredible diversity of birds in North America. It's overwhelming. There are a lot of birds, and many of them look really similar. You may be feeling like you bit off more than you can chew with this whole birding thing, but take a deep breath. Stay calm. Identifying birds can be difficult, to be sure. It can be the subject of scholarly articles and in-depth, jargon-heavy conversation. But don't worry, the vast majority of the birding you'll do isn't as hard as all that. Before long, you'll be comfortable with most of the birds you're likely to see, and what you do about the rest is entirely up to you.

I mentioned before that the birds in your field guide are broken up into groups of closely related species or families. Sometimes this makes sense, as with ducks and geese, gulls and terns. Sometimes it doesn't, as with hawks and falcons. And although those groups appear in separate places throughout the book, the species within each group are very similar. Once you've got an idea what family of birds you're looking at, you're more than halfway there; the rest is a matter of matching the memory of what you've seen to its picture. But getting to that family can be difficult.

This chapter will deal mainly with getting to that point, by accounting for the things that novice birders notice first. They're listed in descending order, from what the novice notices first to what they notice last. Note that this is not always the correct order in which you *should* be thinking when looking at birds.

SIZE—HOW BIG IS IT REALLY?

Is your bird big? Is your bird small? Beginning bird-watchers are prone to putting too much emphasis on the size of a bird when looking at it. Because if you think about it, saying something is "big" or "small" isn't really useful unless you have something to compare it to, and absent that size standard, people have a tendency to over- or underestimate the size of a bird. You know how your uncle always tells exaggerated stories about the fish he caught? The one that was *this big*? You might be doing the same with the bird you saw.

American Robin, American Crow, and Red-Tailed Hawk are abundant continent-wide
and are useful comparisons to anything else you might see.

This is where getting comfortable with your common birds is important. Know
whether something is larger or smaller than an American Robin, an American Crow, or
a Red-Tailed Hawk, to use three common North American species and excellent size
comparisons. You don't need to get out your ruler; you only need to know that your bird
looked smaller than that robin over there but bigger than a chickadee, to get pointed in
the right direction.

Common species useful for size comparison, from smallest to largest:

1. **Hummingbird**–The smallest North American birds,
   some no bigger than large insects. Ruby-Throated
   Hummingbird, at left, is the common species in
   eastern North America.

2. **Chickadee**–All are small, round, and long-tailed. They look like a lollipop with wings, but slightly larger than kinglets and small warblers.

3. **Song Sparrow**–Plump, long-tailed, and common. It's the prototypical sparrow across much of the continent.

4. **Northern Mockingbird**–Prominent across the South, it often perches in conspicuous places making it a great bird to compare with open-country birds. Slender with a long tail.

5. **American Robin**–The ubiquitous lawn thrush.

6. **American Crow**–Loud and large, around the same size as many hawks. If you're confused about a soaring raptor, it's often helpful to compare it to the crow that's probably flying by.

7. **Mallard**–A large and common duck, and a useful size comparison for small, rare geese.

8. **Red-Tailed Hawk**–North America's most common raptor, and one of the larger ones.

9. **Canada Goose**–Everyone knows this golf course denizen. If it's bigger than a Canada Goose, it's probably not a native species of waterfowl—unless it's a swan.

"Slate-Colored" Junco
is the default form in the East.

"Oregon" Junco is a common feeder visitor in
the western part of the continent.

"Red-Backed" Junco is a unique form
restricted to the mountains of southern
Arizona and New Mexico.

These three subspecies of the common Dark-Eyed Junco illustrate how variable color can be.

COLOR—AM I SEEING THINGS?

At first glance, color seems like it would be a great way to identify birds, but I'm here to tell you that your own eyes can, and often will, deceive you. Depending on the angle of the sunlight, the cloud cover, or even your individual eyes, white can look pink, blue can look black, and red can look brown. In one embarrassing situation, I saw a bright white bird look completely black as it flew over the heads of our group of birders on a rainy, overcast morning.

More than that, bird color is so variable, even among birds of the same species. Males and females can be different colors. Birds of different ages can look different. Sometimes, birds will show an absence or presence of pigments in their feathers that makes them abnormally light or dark, and of course, birds show as much or more variation among individuals as people do. If that Northern Cardinal on one side of your yard looks brighter than the other ones, chances are it is. That doesn't make it a different species, though, but novice birders can get thrown off by small differences in plumage color and pattern, and think they're looking at a different species when in fact they're not. Don't fall into this trap.

If you are looking at the colors, focus instead on the patterns. Does the bird have stripes or streaks? Where? Are there blocks of color? These are things that are more consistent and more useful. Color is important, don't get me wrong, and you'll need it. But use color knowing it can be deceiving.

SHAPES AND SILHOUETTES

Instead of color, focus on things that are less variable, like the structure of the bird. Those cardinals may be different shades of red, but they'll always be long-tailed, short-legged, with that peppy crest. In fact, you don't even need the color to identify this bird; the silhouette is that distinctive.

Here are a few more birds with distinctive silhouettes:

1. **Golden-Crowned Kinglet:** More like a ball than a bird. Short wings, short tail, and round body give it a "cute" impression.

2. **White-Breasted Nuthatch:** Subtle in gray, black, and white, these birds often go head-first down the trunk of a tree.

3. **Gadwall:** A plain duck, as far as colors are concerned, but the giant squarish head is obvious even from the other side of a lake.

4. **Cooper's Hawk:** In flight, the long tail, shorter wings, and blocky protruding head give the impression of a flying cross.

HABITAT—IT'S WHERE THEY'RE AT

Now we're getting to the features that really matter. A big part of identifying birds is narrowing down your options from those 900-plus birds in the field guide to a few manageable dozen you can remember. For the most part, birds are nothing if not predictable, particularly with regard to the places they turn up. And knowing what to expect and where to expect it is a *huge* part of making identification easier.

For instance, Sanderling is a very common shorebird often found running with the waves on sandy beaches. You're not going to find it in your backyard (unless your backyard is a beach, of course). Likewise, those Blue Jays picking at peanuts in your backyard are probably not going to be flying around at the beach.

Those are extreme examples, of course. Here's one that is more subtle. In much of the eastern United States and parts of California, both Red-Shouldered Hawks and Red-Tailed Hawks are common, and novice birders occasionally get the two confused, particularly the young birds that have not yet come into their familiar adult plumage. They are different sizes, but remember that size can be hard to determine in a solo bird. Luckily, the two species generally segregate themselves by habitat, with Red-Shouldered Hawks preferring locations with larger trees and often water, and Red-Tailed Hawks liking more open habitats like pastures and fields. This isn't fail-safe, because each can be found in the other's preferred habitat, but the vast majority of the time it works out. So if you see a hawk perched in one of the big trees in your forested backyard in the eastern United States, start with Red-Shouldered and work out from there.

Red-Tailed Hawks prefer open country where it can search for food in flight.

Red-Shouldered Hawks often hunt from a perch in woody areas, seeking snakes and frogs.

Information on habitat preferences, and often on similar species, can be found in the species accounts of your field guide. So don't forget to use those!

See Chapter 9 for examples of habitats where you can find specific groups of birds.

Behavior—What's it Doing?

Individual species of birds mostly look different from one another. This should come as no surprise. But you'll probably be happy to know they act differently too, and paying attention to what a bird is doing can be a really easy way to nail down an identification, even among tough groups of birds. Some birds sit on a branch vertically, with their tail held down. Some sit horizontally, with head and tail on the same plane. Some birds, like many warblers, prefer to hang out in the tops of trees, while others like sparrows, wrens, and thrashers will stay on or close to the ground, often no more than 10 feet (3 m) above the earth. All of these behaviors are clues to be aware of, as in most cases, they will help you narrow those 900-plus species into maybe half a dozen or fewer.

Birds often move in unique ways as well. Novice birders can be easily intimidated by a family as diverse and cryptic as shorebirds, but by paying attention to things like shape, habitat, and particularly behavior, you can become more comfortable with them. For instance, long-legged species like yellowlegs step delicately through shallow waters picking at food on the surface. Dowitchers stand up to their bellies in water, probing the mud with long beaks, looking famously like sewing machines. Plovers employ a run-and-stop approach that distinguishes them from similar-size birds, even at a distance; and Spotted Sandpipers bob their tails up and down like frantic playground seesaws.

In just about all groups of birds, you can narrow down your options by looking at what the birds are doing. And while field guides, with their static images, do not always make these actions obvious, the increasing ease with which birders can take high-quality video with cameras and phones means that video-sharing websites like YouTube and Vimeo are often great places to see birds moving "in the flesh," simply by searching for a specific species. It's an incredibly useful thing to see how a bird moves. In fact, I'm certain that a game-changing video field guide for one's smartphone is only a few years away.

RANGE—NARROWING THINGS DOWN

When birders talk about range, they're talking about where on the map a bird is supposed to be. As I mentioned with habitat, birds are pretty predictable, and for the most part, they stay where they're supposed to be (we'll talk about the exciting exceptions later). Those 900-plus birds in the United States and Canada are not all found together at the same time. A given state or province may host only as many as two hundred or so at any one time.

Most every species in your field guide has a color-coded map associated with it. Some, like American Robin or Red-Tailed Hawk, are found continent-wide at all times of year. Others, like Kirtland's Warbler or Gunnison Sage-Grouse, occupy very small territories and can only be found regularly in certain places.

These maps will clue you in on that information, telling you not only where you can find a given bird, but usually when too. The map should be one of the first places you look when you're trying to identify a bird. It will help you to eliminate a large number of the birds of North America from consideration.

Black-Throated Green Warbler is a common
migrant in the East.

Hermit Warbler breeds in coniferous forests
along the Pacific Coast of North America.

Black-Throated Warbler and Hermit Warbler
are closely related and similar looking, but their
ranges only barely overlap.

ACTIVITY 4:
ASKING FOR HELP

It's also incredibly popular for novice birders to use cameras or smartphones to take pictures of birds and ask for identifications from any of a number of forums, websites, or social media groups. Relatively inexpensive and quality cameras are available to just about anyone nowadays, and many of us carry them around in our pockets constantly in the form of smartphones. It can often be simple to snap identifiable photos of a mystery bird and post them online for more experienced birders to identify for you. Many birders will jump at the opportunity to help a new birder—we all remember when birding was new for us—but there are a couple of unwritten rules regarding social media sharing that you can find yourself violating without knowing it.

1. Seek out groups and forums that are specifically geared toward identification. The people there are more prepared and willing to help out new birders than in a general birding group. Most states and provinces have Facebook groups filled with local birders often willing to help novices with identifications or direct them toward local resources. Finding them is as simple as searching "birding" and your state. For beginners, however, the American Birding Association maintains a couple of groups that are good jumping-off points. You can find them at www.facebook.com/groups/ababirds/ and www.facebook.com/groups/whatsthisbird/

2. It's generally a good idea to take a stab at identifying the bird yourself, before using a social media resource. Explain your reasoning. You can be wildly wrong, it's okay, but it does suggest that you are trying, and the attempt usually goes over well. Plus, you're likely to learn more if you already have a good idea of what to look for.

3. Learn to recognize good advice from bad advice. Birding can be hard, and some identifications can be difficult. When comments start flying in, learn how to pick the wheat from the chaff. For instance, good advice usually includes justification for the answer given. Some individuals have a better track record than others, and typically the opinions of group moderators, the names of whom can be found as a drop-down option in the "Members" tab on Facebook, are worth giving more weight to. This can take time to suss out, however. Online resources can be excellent, but they should supplement, not supplant, a field guide. You learn so much more if you do the leg work yourself.

Apps and Online Resources

With the proliferation of smartphones, many of the major field guide publishers have released app (computer program) versions of their books. It's pretty handy to be able to have all the information available in a 500-page book right in your pocket, and many apps take advantage of the phone speakers to allow recording of bird vocalizations too. In many ways, these apps are better in the field than books for confirming what you're seeing and hearing, but they do have a couple of disadvantages that prevent them from completely replacing a book.

Notably, it's more difficult, though not impossible, to compare species to one another on a phone if you're trying to decide between two or more. Also, if you're completely lost, it's not as easy to flip through the entirety of options. It cannot be denied, however, that apps are incredibly useful and in many cases entirely remove the need to carry a book in the field.

Other resources to help you find what is possible, and what probably isn't, include bird checklists from state or local bird groups, which will usually list only the likely species to be found in the area. Online sites like Avibase and eBird are also good, with the eBird being specific down to the county level.

What is interesting about these lists is that, while a novice birder might consider aspects from the top of this list down when identifying a bird, an experienced birder thinks about range, habitat, and behavior first (the last options on my list). That way, they've already narrowed down the choices to only a handful of species, and they won't get bogged down on what isn't likely. Something to think about as you head into the field.

PHOTOGRAPHS AND SKETCHES

We carry cameras around with us all the time these days in the form of cell phones, and the ability to take a photo of a mystery bird to look at later is a pretty incredible thing when you think about it. Don't be afraid to use your phone, or make a small investment in a point-and-shoot zoom camera to help you with identifying birds. The photos may not be magazine quality, but oftentimes you'll get enough to help jog your memory. Most birders carry around some sort of camera, be it a massive telephoto lens on a Digital SLR or a small pocket zoom. You certainly don't need to spend a lot of money; feel free to experiment with what works for you.

Sometimes birds cannot be identified conclusively in the field, and you need to "bring them with you" to think about them in the comfort of your home with your many field guides. The problem here is that, the further you get away from an encounter, the more your memory of the bird starts to slip. Anyone with a self-administered degree in amateur psychology knows this phenomenon, and with birds, it can be hard to remember all the details. You may want the bird to be something particular—a highly sought-after species or something new for your list—and as time and space grow longer, markings that confused you in the field may now seem conclusive one way or the other. You need a way to objectively consider your mystery bird. If you haven't got the aforementioned pocket camera or other electronic aids, it's time for the field sketch.

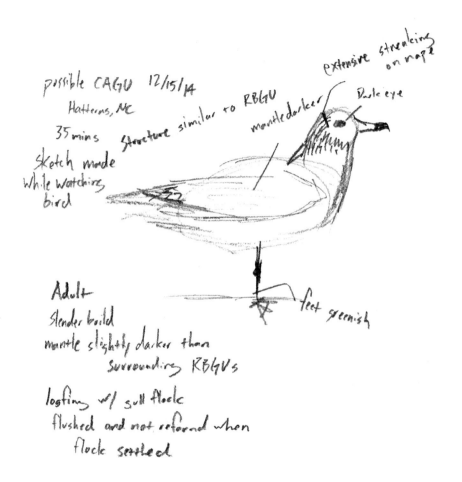

possible CAGU 12/15/14

Hatteras, NC

35 mins

sketch made
while watching
bird

Structure similar to RBGU

mantle darker

extensive streaking
on nape

Dark eye

Adult
slender build
mantle slightly darker than
          surrounding RBGVs

loafing w/ gull flock
flushed and not reformed when
          flock settled

feet greenish

A sketch doesn't have to be a great work of art, as this gull makes clear.
You only need to be able to remember important details.

ACTIVITY 5:
FIELD SKETCHING

Before cameras became so ubiquitous, field sketching was the name of the game. It's just what it sounds like—a quick sketch of a mystery bird, made while you're looking at it, that notes important field marks to help you make an identification later. Field sketches are still really helpful, particularly since a pad of paper and a pencil are far less expensive than even the cheapest camera. Birders might be put off by field sketching because they're uneasy about their artistic skills, but you don't have to be a good artist to make a useful field sketch. You're not making an illustration to hang on your wall, you're making a note of important field marks.

And what's more, making a few sketches helps you to get a good idea of a bird's parts and its posture, both of which can be really important when you're trying to identify a bird.

1. **Find a bird you can watch for a while.** Think about ducks at a pond or a bird visiting your feeders. This will be your subject.

2. **Birds come from eggs.** And so do good bird sketches. Almost all bird bodies are vaguely egg-shaped (round at the front and tapered in the back), so start with an egg oriented the right way and go from there.

3. **Focus on quick and uncomplicated strokes of the pencil.** Don't worry about making it beautiful, you want to impart information to remind yourself of later. Anything not in service of information is excessive. As always, practice makes perfect.

4. **Look for important field marks to focus on.** Things to look for on birds that can be useful for identification include presence/absence of wing-bars, face pattern, leg and feet color, and back pattern. Make sure to note these in your sketch.

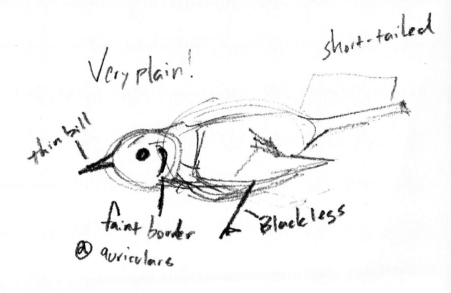

Very plain!

short-tailed

thin bill

faint border
@ auriculars

Blackless

Warbler sp.

Orange Co, NC 10/5/10

Some streaking but faint
Overall grayish
Compact, thin bill

Cape May?

You want field marks that will make figuring out the ID easier when you get back to your book.
Make sure you draw quickly, because the bird could leave at any time.

5. **Don't be afraid to draw parts of the bird separately.** If the wing pattern is particularly notable to you, just draw the wing. If the face is striking, just draw the head.

6. **Focus on patterns and shapes.** Don't worry about individual feathers. Shapes and patterns will be the most useful for identifying what you saw or convincing other people that you saw it.

Sketching common birds will help you understand the important parts of the bird. Not only will this help you identify common species but, in the event you find something really unusual, you'll be able to document it thoroughly and better convince other birders of what you saw.

Chapter 5

BIRDING IS BETTER WITH FRIENDS

One of the most rewarding aspects of birding is that there are so many opportunities to share the experience with like-minded individuals. The culture of birding is such that sharing information and knowledge is encouraged, and that makes it really easy for a new birder to quickly get up to speed if they're willing to put a little work in.

Just about every town of any size in the United States or Canada has an Audubon Society or a bird club, or both. Most bird clubs offer free monthly meetings that feature a meet-and-greet and a guest speaker. Popular topics include recent birding trips to various exotic places or local conservation initiatives, but any nature-themed topic is explored, and the topics usually are planned out well in advance and posted on the organization's website. In addition to meetings, most bird clubs host weekly or semi-weekly bird walks to a local hotspot. These walks are typically led by an experienced birder and held to appeal to novices. The pace is generally easy and appropriate for people getting into birds for the first time, but is also largely dependent on the size of the group—large groups tend to move more slowly than small ones.

There is really no better way to get comfortable with the skills required to be a good birder and, indeed, with the culture of birding, than to take advantage of one of these bird walks. As with anything that puts a number of different people in one place, conflicts can emerge. Most of these have to do with misunderstanding the unwritten "rules" of bird walks. Depending on the leader, those might be spelled out or left unsaid. But in order to make the most of your time in the field, try to abide by the following best practices.

When birding in groups, make sure you pay attention to the leader and share optics with everybody.

THINGS TO CONSIDER WHEN GOING ON A BIRD WALK

1. **Don't Be Late!** Most bird walks take place in the morning, which, admittedly, is not always convenient, but it's generally the best time for encountering active birds. Most walks split the difference between accommodating both birds and birders, and will start between eight and nine in the morning, so time spent waiting around for people to arrive is time taken away from peak bird activity. Try to arrive a little early because that time is usually spent arranging carpool options and making sure rules and roles are clarified.

2. **Know the Leader.** If there's something you particularly want to see or something you particularly want to know, be sure to make the leader aware. Most leaders will be happy to accommodate the needs of the participants, if they know about them.

3. **Try Not to Talk *Too* Much.** We are social creatures, we humans, and asking for complete silence on a bird walk is asking way too much. But a leader relies on hearing to find most of the birds for the group, and when people are talking too much, it becomes difficult for them to do their job. Socializing with other birders is one of the wonderful things about this hobby, but make sure there's a time and a place for it. When hanging around after the walk? Absolutely. While walking along a hedgerow? Probably not.

4. **Don't Be a Scope Hog.** Many times, a leader or one of the participants will bring along a spotting scope to give up-close looks at the birds you seek. With only a few scopes for an entire group, it's important to think about scope etiquette when the bird is teed up. A good leader will find the bird in the scope then quickly back away for participants to enjoy the bird. The general rule is for participants to make a line and take a few seconds (no more than five) to watch the bird before stepping aside for the next in line. This is so that everybody gets a chance to see the target bird before it flies away. If, after everyone has seen it, the bird is still in the scope view, then you can take a longer look, or even try to take a photo through the scope with a camera or cell phone.

5. **Manage Your Expectations.** Birding is nothing if not humbling, and the longer you do it, the more humbling it becomes. Sometimes the birding is phenomenal, with birds dripping off the trees and filling scopes and binoculars with crushing views. Other times there's just not a lot going on. Sometimes the bird you really want to see flies off, out of scope view and over the hill right before you get to see it. Birding is wonderful, but it can be frustrating. Appreciate the magical times when they come, because they aren't always here.

BIRDING GROUPS BEYOND YOUR BACKYARD

Once you've become familiar with your local bird club, you may want to become more involved in bird groups with a scope bigger than your town or region. You might even be interested in exploring the birding opportunities in your state or province, which can be especially exciting. State and provincial birding clubs are an excellent place to go next, because you'll meet and bird with people from a much wider area.

Most state/provincial bird clubs will maintain, or at least be closely associated with, an email listserv or forum. Listserv sites have played a pretty important role in building statewide or regional birding communities. They're invaluable places to share information, report rare or noteworthy birds, or facilitate bird-related activism. Granted, email lists have their cons as well, not least of which is that you might be getting unwanted emails and encountering various Internet etiquette issues, but that's nothing a good sense of humor and judicious use of the "delete" function can't solve. State or provincial birding clubs often host meetings annually or even several times a year, where birders can gather at a statewide hotspot, participate in field trips, and listen to talks by experts. These tend to be pretty fun affairs, and further the opportunity to learn from and meet interesting people.

National organizations, like the American Birding Association (ABA) and Audubon, are primarily advocacy groups rather than social organizations, but the ABA does host events at national and international birding hotspots and is active in social media, rare-bird reporting, and birding ethics. Audubon is an international conservation organization with a focus on birds. Both produce excellent periodicals for members and are well worth joining to supplement your birding experience.

ACTIVITY 6:
GO ON A BIRD WALK

Grab your binoculars and head out into the field with some like-minded birders. There's really no better way to build your birding skills than by going birding with those more skilled than you.

The best walks aimed at novice birders are usually those run by bird supply stores, local bird clubs, or Audubon society chapters. These are great places for experienced birders new to an area to get involved in the local community too. My own first birding experiences in my hometown were via walks led by a nearby bird supply store.

Finding a local bird club can be as easy as plugging "Bird Club plus (your town)" into Google, but the National Audubon Society has also made it easy by creating a database that contains all their local chapters across the continent. You can find it at www.audubon.org/search-by-zip. Enter your zip code, and you're ready to go. Most keep a calendar that shows when and where a bird walk is occurring. Walks will either meet at a designated birding location at a certain time, or they'll meet at a local meet-up spot and carpool.

Try to remember the tips listed earlier in this chapter when you're out in the field. It's not a bad idea to bring a field guide along but try not to get your head stuck in it the whole time. Talking to birders about what they're seeing and what they're thinking when they're trying to identify a bird—particularly when that bird is right in front of you—is really the best way to learn. You can always cross-check that advice against your guide later. Questions are expected, but remember to try to hold your discussion to when the leader is not actively searching for birds.

Dress for the weather and wear comfortable shoes, and I can guarantee you'll have a great time whether or not the birding is great.

Who knows? You may find yourself involved in a great group of local conservationists and hobbyists with whom you'll spend lots of exciting time in the field and with the birds.

Chapter 6

BRINGING THE BIRDS HOME

For many birders, the easiest way to interact with birds is by setting up a feeding station in your yard. There are any number of books that deal with this in great detail, and it isn't my intention to repeat that wealth of information, but only to provide a framework for understanding the basics of bird feeding. A birder visiting a bird supply store can easily go down the rabbit hole and end up susceptible to an impressive array of options, some more elaborate than are necessary, and some just slick marketing. In the end, bird feeding is pretty simple, and you don't have to do a lot to attract a good variety of birds to your yard.

It's important to note that feeding birds is an activity done solely for the sake of the bird-watcher, not the bird. Birds are hardy animals despite their size, and are remarkably adept at finding food for themselves. Typically, a bird will get only a small portion of its daily intake from bird feeders, and while birds will certainly take advantage of the food left out for them, a birder shouldn't feel guilty for not feeding birds or failing to feed birds year round. The food brings the birds in so you can see them, and that's certainly great, but they very rarely will depend on it for their survival, even in the most difficult weather.

CHARACTERISTICS OF A BIRD-FRIENDLY YARD

Not all yards are created equal. Not every person lives in a neighborhood with established trees, or one that backs up to a marsh, or one that lies along a migration corridor. We must make do with what we have. That said, rural yards tend to attract more birds than urban yards. Neighborhoods with established trees nearby tend to attract more birds than new neighborhoods. And proximity to water is always a plus. These things are mostly out of your control.

What you can control are the types of food you offer and the feeders you put it in, the presence of cover, and the types of plants you put in your yard. We'll cover each of these in turn.

A bird-friendly yard generally contains three characteristics: food, water, and places where a bird can hide. Well-placed nest boxes can also attract cavity nesting birds like bluebirds, chickadees, or nuthatches.

BIRDING WITH THE BOSS

Offering quality food in your yard is the single most-effective thing you can do to bring in a diverse assemblage of birds. By that, I mean making an effort to get the good stuff at a bird supply store and not the bags of mixed seed at the local supermarket. Yes, the former tends to be more expensive, but that's largely because supermarket bird food contains mostly filler seed that is unattractive to most native bird species. They simply won't touch it, and if you put out cheap bird food, you might notice that the birds will pick out the good stuff and leave you with a feeder full of crap seed that even European Starlings won't touch.

If you're only going to feed one type of seed out of one feeder, make sure that seed is black oil sunflower seed (BOSS). There is no alternative if you want to bring birds to your feeder. BOSS is high in fat content, which for birds means energy, and pound for pound, there's no other seed like it. Many species of birds will readily come to a feeder stocked with BOSS, and each attacks the kernels in its own way. Cardinals and grosbeaks will crush the seeds whole with their massive beaks. Chickadees and titmice will grab a seed and take it to a nearby branch to hold it between their feet and break it open with their chisel bills. Nuthatches will wedge the seed in a crevice in the bark and whale on it like a hammer on an anvil. Many sparrows will be content to hop around underneath picking up scraps. It's fascinating to watch, and it helps you in the field by giving you insight into bird behavior.

You may also see striped sunflower seeds available. They attract many of the same species, but because the shells tend to be thicker, some of the smaller birds may have trouble with them, and so it's not as good for attracting a wide variety of birds.

Birds are only interested in the "meat" of the seed, the fatty kernel inside, and birds like cardinals and grosbeaks will shuck sunflower seeds with gusto as they pick them up, leaving the shells to pile up beneath the feeder. Birders unwilling to deal with the mess can also buy shelled sunflower seeds, but these tend to be more expensive and can spoil if left unattended.

BOSS seeds can be distributed in just about any type of feeder except for those with very small openings, which are made specifically for the next type of seed.

Nyjer—Black Gold

If you feed two types of seeds, the second should be nyjer, or niger (nī-jer). Often referred to as thistle seed, this extremely small and thin seed has no peer when the goal is to attract finches, which will readily come to it. Imported from Africa and Asia, it tends to be more expensive, which is why it's usually set out in a tube feeder or sack with small holes to exclude larger birds who will devour it if given the chance. Nyjer is an excellent option in the winter months when birders are looking to attract irruptive finches from the North like Pine Siskins and redpolls.

A tube feeder holding nyjer seeds
is a magnet for finches, like these
Pine Siskins.

MILLET FOR THE GROUND FEEDERS

Millet is a small round seed that is often part of mixed-seed bags but can also be purchased on its own. It's particularly good for ground-feeding birds like sparrows, buntings, and doves, which will come to it if it's scattered around or on a table feeder not more than a few inches off the ground.

NUTS, WORMS, AND OTHER SEEDS

Once you get beyond the three seeds mentioned above, you've entered the realm of the specialty bird feeder. The types of food you can offer at a feeding station in your yard are myriad, and while you don't need to feel as though you must offer a smorgasbord for the birds in your yard, you certainly can if you're willing to shoulder the trouble and the expense.

Peanuts are a popular food for jays and woodpeckers, who will take them readily. Safflower is a large white seed that attracts many of the same species as BOSS but without the often undesirable and gluttonous grackles, starlings, and blackbirds, and is an option if your yard is overrun by those species. Birders will even purchase mealworms for insect-eating species that are less inclined to visit seed feeders. As with everything else, these foods are most effective at attracting birds in the winter months, when they are looking to supplement their natural diets with high-fat and high-protein options.

Have Your Cake, They'll Eat it Too

Suet, rendered and solidified animal fat, is also a popular food at the feeding station, particularly among woodpeckers, chickadees, and titmouses. It can also attract birds that are not seed-eaters, like mockingbirds, thrashers, and bluebirds. The suet is usually in the form of a square cake and put into a small metal cage for birds to cling to. You can hang it from just about anywhere. Loose suet can also be crammed into crevices and tree bark for woodpeckers and nuthatches to find.

ACTIVITY 7:
MAKING SUET

Suet is rendered fat usually molded into a square. A wide variety of birds are attracted to it, including those that would not typically come to a seed feeder.

You can purchase suet cakes at a bird supply store, but they're just as easy to make yourself. You can use actual suet from a butcher if you have access to it, but lard, bacon fat, peanut butter, or any combination of the three, works just as well. The name of the game is fat, which is energy for a bird, so try to avoid adding sugars or bread. Note that none of this is set in stone, and you can easily mix the proportions up, based on how solid you want the end result to be. So long as it's at least semi-solid, the birds will eat it up.

Here's my recipe:

1. Ingredients are 2 parts fat (lard, bacon fat, or peanut butter), 2 parts cornmeal or oatmeal to hold the mixture together, 1 part "extras."

2. Melt the fat over a stovetop, and add the cornmeal/oatmeal.

3. Feel free to throw in some extras. I often add a handful of BOSS to my mix, and others might add dried fruit or freeze-dried mealworms. It's up to you.

4. If you have problems with squirrels eating your suet, you can add a healthy dose of hot sauce or cayenne pepper at this point to ward them off. They'll quickly learn to leave it alone, and it doesn't bother the birds because they lack taste buds.

5. Pour the mixture into molds. These can be washed out tuna cans, square Tupperware containers, or whatever you have around. I usually buy a couple suet cakes at the bird store and keep the plastic molds they come in so I can re-use them with the homemade stuff. Put the suet cakes in the freezer until they firm up, usually around twenty-four hours.

6. Pop them out and throw them in the suet cage. The birds will be right along.

SUMMER FEEDING:
HUMMINGBIRDS AND ORIOLES

Feeding hummingbirds is a special case, and generally the only feeding you might feel like you want to do in the summer—they're a blast to have around. Any sort of hummingbird feeder will do, but you might want to purchase one with insect guards, because the birds are not the only ones who will take advantage of the sugar water.

It's important to remember that you do not need to dye the sugar-water mixture red. While hummingbirds are certainly attracted to the color red, the feeder itself will do that job. All the birds need is sugar water, and the red food coloring could potentially harm them. You don't need it, so don't worry about it.

The ideal mixture of sugar to water is one to four. So one cup of sugar needs to be dissolved in four cups of water. Mix it up thoroughly (warming the water in the microwave a bit helps), and fill as much as you need. Try to replace the water every four to five days regardless of how much is used, to prevent it from fermenting and growing mold. Clean the feeder regularly with dish soap and rinse it well.

Depending on where you live on the continent, hummingbirds will arrive in late March or early April and will depart by October. Some parts of the southern tier of the United States are fortunate to have them year round, however, and in the East especially, it is becoming common for birders to leave their feeders out into the winter in the hopes a rare vagrant will show up. The western breeding Rufous Hummingbird has become a rare but annual visitor across the East in the past decade, and other vagrants are possible as well.

Keep a close eye on the birds at your feeder, know your common species well, and be prepared to snap a photo or make a quick sketch if something unusual comes along.

You can hang a hummingbird feeder near a window so you can watch the show.
Hummingbirds can be fearless and will soon get used to your prescence.

LANDSCAPING FOR BIRDS

Landscaping for birds is simply making sure that they have opportunities for food, water and shelter in your yard. These can be as elaborate as a well-maintained hummingbird garden with a flowing water feature or as simple as a birdbath and a brush pile.

Water is a nice supplement to a feeding station, and birds may come to visit it every day to bathe and drink. A feature that drips or bubbles will likely draw a bird's attention, but isn't necessary. Particularly in colder months, when open water is scarce, birds might be more attracted to the water than the food. In cases like that, a small electric heater can be added to keep the water free of ice.

A garden or yard that includes fruiting shrubs and trees is probably the best thing you can do to attract birds regularly to your yard. I always encourage the planting of Flowering Dogwoods, particularly in the East, as they are prolific fruiters that birds will swarm to in the fall. In addition, they are attractive trees in their own right, particularly in early spring when they're in bloom. When choosing fruiting trees, try hard to choose native species rather than introduced ones. Birds are excellent distributers of tree seeds, as anyone with a newly washed car can attest to, and it's far better to spread the seeds of native trees far and wide than those of potentially ecologically destructive introduced species. Trees like dogwood, American holly, hackberry, chokecherry, and others are good. Privet, autumn olive, and others are not. Make sure you do your research. The local ecosystem will be better for it, and the birds couldn't care less.

For attracting hummingbirds to your garden, look to plant flowers that have long tubes. Trumpet creeper, bee balm, and salvia are excellent choices, depending on where you live and what you can grow, but anything colorful will usually do the trick. The hummingbirds will be as attracted to the bugs that visit the flowers as to the nectar itself—growing chicks need protein.

Your local bird supply store can be a great resource for more-detailed information than provided in this cursory overview. Be sure to ask for their opinions on bird feeding and managing your property for bird diversity.

ACTIVITY 8:
BUILD A BIRD–FRIENDLY YARD

If you've got space on your property for feeders, you'll probably want to make sure that the largest diversity of birds will be using them. Most people with bird-friendly yards consider the development of such to be a continual ongoing project, rather than a one-time setup. After all, some shrubs take time to grow, and if you have fun with it, you'll probably add aspects to your feeding station continually as you bring in more and more specialized bird species.

Your focus should be on these things in this order:

1. **Food** – Find a tree or stand to set up at least one, perhaps two, bird feeders. Remember, black-oil sunflower seed is the best if you're going to stay with one seed, and a simple hopper-type feeder—hung from a tree branch or stand and filled with the BOSS—is best if you're going to stick with one feeder. If you add a second food source, try nyjer or homemade suet. The feeders can be placed relatively close together; most birds in the winter are tolerant of other individuals and species, so there's no need to spread them out. Long-term projects can include planting bird-friendly trees and shrubs like dogwood or beautyberry. These may take time to mature, but once they're fruiting, they offer a steady supply of bird food that you don't have to worry about replenishing every week.

2. **Shelter** – A brush pile near the feeding station will make your birds comfortable, and you'll likely see more individuals visiting your feeders. The brush pile can be branches from tree-trimming or even old Christmas trees. If you're hesitant to make your yard look like a compost pile, however, you can plant some shrubs nearby or locate your feeder near existing trees or shrubs. Some secretive species will appreciate having a place to disappear into in a nervous moment, and the birds will be safer from the occasional hawk strafing as well.

A bird-friendly yard usually offers a variety of food and some soft cover for shy species.
Water features and houses are great, but they are not required.

3. **Water** – As mentioned earlier, water is a nice supplement to your feeding station, particularly for birds that don't eat seeds. A classic pedestal birdbath is sufficient, but if you can add a moving-water feature to it, it will be more attractive. This can be a drip or spray feature that attaches to a hose, or something as simple as a milk jug with a pin hole, suspended over the water.

Feel free to experiment. If you're lucky, you may never even need to leave home to see an incredible array of birds.

ACTIVITY 8.5:
BIRD HOUSE
DO'S AND DON'TS

Feeding birds isn't the only way you can welcome them to your yard; you can also provide nest boxes and watch birds grow up right outside your window.

You can build your own nest boxes, but I've never felt the need to go to that kind of trouble. Generally, your local birding supply store will have a selection of boxes, some of which may have been built by local craftsmen. Local Audubon chapters will occasionally sell nest boxes as a fund-raiser, and Boy Scout troops will make boxes for badges or fund-raisers as well. I prefer these options to making my own, because I always feel better knowing my money is going to a worthy cause.

Generally, nest boxes are attractive to those species that use abandoned woodpecker holes, which is only a handful of species in North America. The types of species you are likely to attract are entirely dependent on two criteria: the size of the hole and the surrounding habitat.

Many wrens will readily take to nest boxes, but also eaves, gas grills, or any other sheltered cavity.

To attract the following species, consider these things:

1. **House Wren**: This unassuming little brown bird with the glorious song prefers boxes with a hole ⅞ inch (2.2 cm) in diameter—the size of a quarter. Most decorative "house"-style birdhouses are made with House Wrens in mind. Place the house no more than 10 feet (3 m) off the ground and near brushy and shrubby habitats.

2. **Chickadee, Titmouse, Nuthatch**: These three woodland species prefer boxes with a 1⅛-inch (2.9 cm) hole, but will use boxes with larger holes when available. Boxes placed in wooded lots or in forests, and no more than 15 feet (4.6 m) off the ground, will likely be used by these species.

3. **Bluebird**: The story of the Eastern Bluebird is one of the great conservation success stories in North America—made possible largely by the proliferation of nest boxes. The three species of bluebirds in North America all prefer boxes placed in an open area with holes about 1½ inches (3.8 cm) in diameter. Boxes in parks, pasturelands, and golf courses are all likely to be used, and should be placed 3 to 6 feet (0.9 to 1.8 m) off the ground.

4. **Screech Owl**: Owls are cool enough, but imagine having them in your own yard. These small owls prefer boxes with 3-inch (7.6-cm) holes and wood shavings at the bottom—they don't make much of a nest. Place the boxes at least 10 feet (3 m) off the ground in wooded clearings or near stream edges.

5. **Wood Duck, Goldeneye, Hooded Merganser**: These three species of ducks also nest in tree cavities, and all prefer large boxes with a 4-inch-diameter (10.2-cm) hole. You can place the box either on a tree overlooking a quiet pond or swamp, or on a pole in the middle of the pond.

Chapter 7

BIRDING AS GIVING:
CITIZEN SCIENCE

One of the wonderful things about being a birder is that ornithology remains one of the very few sciences in which amateurs can have a significant impact on real science. There are no hobby particle-physicists, no armchair organic-chemists, but birders are able to provide great data to those who actively study bird distribution and abundance, simply by going out into the field and recording what they see. And this is easier than it ever has been, thanks to the Internet, social media, and the ability of birders to easily communicate with others around the world. This is nothing new though. In fact, hobby birders have had a long history of contributing to science—from the moment binoculars were placed in our hands.

In 1900, an ornithologist named Frank Chapman, an officer in the newly organized Audubon Society, was concerned with declining bird populations. In recent years, Passenger Pigeons and Carolina Parakeets, both formerly abundant species in North America, had seen drastic declines. In both cases, the birds were near extinction, a seemingly impossible result for two species that were famously abundant. Flocks of Passenger Pigeons were said to have taken hours to pass overhead, and there were so many Carolina Parakeets that the flocks struck fear into the owners of fruit orchards across the southeast United States. By 1900, both were almost completely gone, and Chapman and his colleagues at the Audubon Society were worried.

In the late 1800s, it was popular for naturalists to engage in an activity known as a "side hunt." Participants would choose a day in late December around the holiday season, head out with their shotguns, and compete to bring home the biggest pile of birds (and mammals). Chapman wanted to change that, so he proposed a new activity, by which bird-watchers would travel afield on a chosen day around the end of December or the beginning of January, and seek to count all the birds they saw. He called it the Christmas Bird Count (CBC), and twenty-five counts were held that first year, from Ontario to California.

Since Chapman's first CBC in 1900, the activity has grown to an annual event that takes places around the world. In 2008, there were more than 2,000 counts with nearly 60,000 participants. The numbers are only increasing.

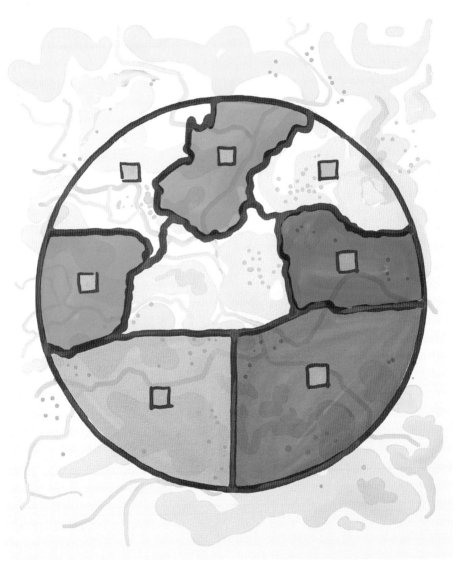

A Christmas Bird Count circle is 15 miles (24 km) in diameter, and often split into smaller regions.
A birder or team of birders will each take a region to ensure full coverage.

CHRISTMAS BIRD COUNT—THE BASICS

In concept, the Christmas Bird Count is pretty simple. From a random point on the map, you draw a circle with a radius of 7½ miles (12 km). You, a group of birders, or many dozens of birders, attempt to count every single bird within that circle. With large and well-established counts, the circle will usually be broken up into several regions with groups of birders tackling specific regions, so as not to overlap each other and count birds twice. And when you count birds, you count every single bird. Numbers are important to determine whether populations are decreasing, increasing, or remaining the same. As you might expect, over many years, things can change quite a bit inside the circle, but that circle remains the same. And that's the key to the CBC's scientific power: You're sampling the same place, year after year after year.

That's the scientific justification for CBCs, but the truth of the matter is that CBCs are flat-out fun. They're a great way to learn about the birds in your area and a great way to meet a lot of dedicated birders. Most CBC compilers (the term given to the person who runs the count in a given year) will be very accommodating about setting novice birders up with an experienced partner. The time commitment runs the gamut from a dawn-to-dusk run to a few spare hours, so you can participate to the extent that your schedule allows. Rural counts tend to have fewer counters than urban counts, but some seemingly out-of-the-way counts are big draws for experienced birders because the potential for great birding is so good.

Most CBCs also host some sort of countdown event in the evening. These are often pot-luck affairs at a participant's home, the highlight of which is the compilation, in which every group gets to announce their species and numbers, and the compiler puts together the totals for the entire count circle. It may sound cheesy, but there's nothing like a room brought to surprise when someone pulls out something really good. If you participate in a count, make sure your first is one with a well-attended compilation party.

Breeding Bird Surveys

In addition to the Christmas Bird Count, the next-longest-running citizen science initiative is the Breeding Bird Survey (BBS). Like the CBC, the value of the BBS is that you are surveying the same area again and again over several years, determining changes in distribution and abundance of breeding birds.

A Breeding Bird Survey consists of a 24½-mile (40 km) route. In late spring and early summer, after the last migratory birds have gone north, the birder drives the route, stopping every half mile to perform a 3-minute point count. Essentially, every half mile a birder stops, counts everything they see and hear for three minutes, and makes a note of the species and numbers.

Unlike the CBC, a Breeding Bird Survey is a more solitary affair, though groups of birders can participate. It requires a bit more skill, because the ability to identify birds by their vocalizations is critically important. That shouldn't stop anyone from wanting to participate, however, and even though available routes infrequently come up, they're critical to our understanding of changes to bird populations.

A birder on a BBS route traverses a 24.5-mile (40 km) route, stopping every half mile (0.8 km) to count every bird they see or hear.

eBird—The Citizen Science Project That Binds Them All

The very best citizen science initiatives offer something for the birder, too. And in that arena, there is truly no better program for birds and birders than eBird. I am an unapologetic eBird evangelical, and I use the website for just about every aspect of my own birding, from personal record-keeping to researching birding locations, to finding answers to status and distribution questions. And in addition to all these offerings for the birder, the remarkable thing about eBird is that the lists birders keep are making important contributions to our understanding of bird populations. But I get ahead of myself; here's the skinny on eBird.

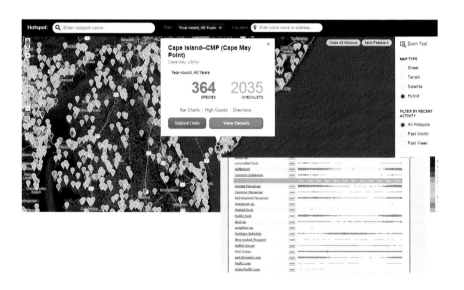

A joint project by the Cornell Lab of Ornithology and Audubon, eBird is a web-based program designed to keep track of the birds people encounter when they're out birding. It's sort of like the Christmas Bird Count in that birders are encouraged to count everything they find, but it's not limited to a specific location or a specific period of time as with the CBC. The interface is fairly intuitive. First, birders use a map to geo-locate where they went birding on a particular day. (Most popular birding locations already exist as "hotspots.") They're then prompted to estimate how long they spent birding and how far they traveled; precision is appreciated but not required. Then the birder simply enters the species and numbers of birds they found on that outing. It's that simple, and you can do it for any spot on the globe.

The magic of eBird comes in what it does with those numbers. Your checklists are combined with the many thousands of other birders' lists to get a snapshot, one that's constantly moving and changing, of bird populations worldwide. This is all wonderful for the scientists who intend to use this data, but for the birder, what it means is that you have a record of all of your sightings, categorized by location (county, state, country, world, etc.) and freely available to you anywhere you have access to the Internet.

And more, you have access to everyone else's sightings too. Imagine you're traveling to California, and you're interested in finding the very localized California Gnatcatcher. A quick look at eBird gives you the locations and dates of every recent California Gnatcatcher sighting, giving you the kind of information that will help you to see this bird.

You might wonder about the validity of the sightings; after all, birding is difficult, and mistakes can be made. But for every region, a volunteer reviewer is tasked with looking at unusual sightings and verifying them with the observer. What this means for the person making the sighting is that, once you are a regular eBird user, you might get a form email asking you for more information or a photo. It's important to note that this is a pretty standard occurrence in the birding world, and most of the time, the reviewer is only looking for a short description of what you saw. If you're correct in your identification, the report will be summarily accepted. If you're not, the reviewer will usually be happy to help you find the right ID. It's important to note that this sort of inquiry is not personal, but done only in the interest of making sure the database is as correct as possible.

And that database is critical for the real science being done with eBird data. Because the checklists are for all parts of the globe and for all times of the year, fluctuations in bird populations are made more obvious, and the information gathered with regard to distribution is critical for assessing the need to protect very specific sites that birds may rely on in migration or during the non-breeding season. The CBCs and BBSs have been extremely important in providing information over the years, but a program like eBird fills in the gaps in our knowledge that still remain.

ACTIVITY 9:
GET eBIRDING

I could write a chapter about eBird on its own, because it's such an incredible tool and has been a true game-changer for birding worldwide. But there's only so much I can explain. I would urge anyone reading this book to set up an account at eBird.org and begin entering checklists, even from your backyard. Every little bit counts, and it's tons of fun, too.

Some tips for submitting the highest-quality data:

1. **Use hotspots!** – Most publicly accessible birding sites are already entered into eBird as a "hotspot." When you visit one of these sites, be sure to use that existing hotspot so that your data will be included with all the other data collected there.

2. **Be specific!** – If you're not using a hotspot, try to place the locator point as close to the actual site as possible. Placing a point on your house or your street will be good for all your feeder birds.

3. **Count carefully, but conservatively!** – eBird asks that you count every individual of every species, but that can be hard. Estimates are okay, but try to err on the side of being conservative rather than looking to post the big numbers.

4. **Leave comments!** – If you see something unusual, make sure you mention what you saw and how you know what you saw. One of the great advantages of eBird is the system of over 500 local reviewers who effectively do quality control on the data, double-checking everything that goes into the database. If you receive an email from them asking about a particular sighting, don't take it personally. This system of checks and verification is common in the birding community, so it's important to get familiar with it. If you have photos, field notes, or sketches, just send them along, and the reviewers can either accept your sighting or help you get it right.

5. **eBird everywhere!** – Mobile technology has made eBird easier than ever. BirdLog is an app for your smartphone that allows you to enter eBird checklists from the field, with no need to sit down and do it afterward. It automatically determines your location using your phone's global positioning system (GPS) and either connects you with hotspots or puts a pin precisely where you are. With BirdLog, there's no reason not to be eBirding! And your incidental data is, in many ways, as important as anything else in determining where birds are and how many there are.

The incredible thing about eBird is that it has managed to split the difference between birding for yourself and birding for a greater cause. It takes all the birding you do—seeing new birds or visiting new places in your area or around the world—and it keeps track of all your records while making that important data available to scientists who need it to learn about bird populations. If you take one thing from this book, I hope you will be encouraged to use eBird and let the birding you do make a difference beyond the intrinsic value it has for you as an individual.

Like many birders, I would seek out birds and keep track of them without eBird, but I love knowing that I'm helping, even when I'm birding for myself.

Chapter 8

FIELD CRAFT:
TIPS FOR FINDING BIRDS IN THE FIELD

When you first start birding, finding birds in the field is as easy as looking out your back door. But it doesn't take long before you realize that 90 percent of the birds you see tend to be the same species, over and over. To find more unusual ones, perhaps birds you've circled in your field guide, you've got to get out and start looking. Focusing your attention on certain pockets of good habitat or certain times of year is a good bet, but each family of birds requires a different strategy for finding them. This chapter seeks to give you tips for seeking out different groups of birds. Note that there is significant overlap between some of them, and a good place for one type of bird is likely to be a good place overall. But finding some families of birds requires a certain way of looking, and I want to give you advice from one who has some experience.

Finding Waterfowl

Finding ducks, geese, and other water birds seems like it's as easy as heading to the nearest park with a bag of stale bread, but unless you want to look at a bunch of weird mutt Mallards, there are better ways to go.

Most waterfowl in North America (and around the world for that matter) are highly migratory. For the warm parts of the year, they're tucked away on ponds on the Great Plains of Canada and northern United States, raising the next generation. Some even breed in the high arctic regions, where they take advantage of the short but productive arctic summer. Even those few species that breed in places where birders in the Lower 48 and southern Canada are likely to see them, dissolve into the wilds in summer. If you want to see the diverse, bizarre, and fantastic assemblage of waterfowl in North America, you're going to have to wait till winter. That's when that stuff gets fun.

It perhaps goes without saying that to find waterfowl, you need to find water. But not all water is the same. Ducks can be roughly broken down into two categories: dabbling ducks, which are your typical broad-billed puddle ducks with the tipping-over foraging technique and familiar quack; and diving ducks, which are typically smaller, more subdued in plumage, and as the name suggests, dive for vegetation and small animals they find on the bottom of ponds and lakes. While either can be found anywhere, the dabblers generally prefer shallower ponds and marshes while the divers will usually be found in deeper water.

Black-Necked Stilts (back) and American Avocets (front) are both long-legged shorebirds. They wade in deeper water than other species.

Sea ducks are those species, like eiders and scoters, that prefer saltwater to fresh. While they can be found far out on the ocean, they're usually within sight of land. They occasionally bunch up in large flocks called "rafts" that can look like a distant oil slick. These ducks are present generally all along the coast in some numbers, but concentrations of them can be found near rocky jetties or tucked away out of the wind on protected bays.

Ducks tend to gather in large mixed flocks in the winter, and it's not uncommon to find a number of species together in one large group. Even flocks of those aforementioned mutt Mallards at the park can occasionally host wild birds, and this can be a good opportunity to study those wild birds closely, as even normally skittish individuals can take on the demeanor of the pushy semi-domestic birds. Geese can do this too, as those flocks of annoying non-migratory Canada Geese that hang out on golf courses or on neighborhood ponds can attract unusual species from time to time, particularly in the winter. In the northeastern United States, even rare European species like Barnacle Goose and Pink-Footed Goose will take up with the park Canada Geese, so it pays to look at something familiar to find something different.

While nearly every pond or lake of a certain size will host a few birds, the very best places to find good varieties of waterfowl are national wildlife refuges, particularly those in the southern or coastal United States. Duck hunting is popular in these places, and the refuges are often specifically managed for ducks and geese. Good places for large congregations of waterfowl in the winter include Merritt Island National Wildlife

Refuge (NWR) in Florida, Lake Mattamuskeet NWR in North Carolina, Bosque del Apache NWR in New Mexico, and Klamath Basin NWR complex in northern California and southern Oregon. And there's almost certainly one near you, wherever you are, that is similarly packed with birds. In the right places, waterfowl are hard to miss.

Tips to remember:

1. Find open water when all other waters are frozen over.

2. Make sure to check the common species for less-common ones.

3. Spring, fall, and winter are the best seasons for finding waterfowl.

4. Males and females of many species look very different, but structurally they will be similar. Before thinking you've found a rare bird, make sure you're not looking at a female of a common species.

Other Birds to Look for When You're Looking for Waterfowl: Ponds, marshes, and lakes tend to be great places for birds generally, because there's a lot of food to take advantage of there. When looking for waterfowl, be on the lookout for other diving birds like loons, grebes, and cormorants, or dabbling birds like coots. They share many of the same habitats and behaviors.

Along the margins, long-legged wading birds like herons, egrets, and ibis roam. The larger birds will prefer deeper water, and the smaller ones will hide in stands of dense vegetation along the shoreline.

Birders at a hawkwatch stay in one place and count every hawk, eagle, or falcon that passes by their spot.

Finding Raptors

There are few groups of birds that are as fascinating, even to non-birders, as raptors. Maybe it's the fierce demeanor, maybe it's the appeal of the hunter, maybe people love that little bit of implied danger. Raptors are big and charismatic, and, even among serious birders, there are those who focus on raptors at the expense of all else.

Finding raptors isn't too difficult, because they're conspicuous when the weather is right. Big soaring raptors like Red-Tailed Hawks and vultures get up in the air when the sun is out, and can easily be seen overhead, seeking food over neighborhoods or even big cities just about any time of the year. Small bird-eating hawks like Sharp-Shinned and Cooper's hawks will strafe feeding stations, proving that the birds at the feeders are as much a draw as the seed you put out.

For variety of raptors, you can't beat a hawk watch on a fall afternoon. Hawks migrate during the day, and follow well-known geographic landmarks to orient themselves. A hawk watch is nothing more than a publicly accessible location where birders gather to watch raptors go by. Depending on the weather and where the hawk watch is located, a birder could see a dozen species over the course of a day, including hawks, vultures, eagles, and falcons.

Because raptors are predators, other birds are often very attuned to their presence, and you can often find a raptor by paying attention to the behavior of other birds. For instance, small flocks of chickadees and titmice will often harass a perched raptor they find until they force it away. Any sort of uproar with chickadees in the center of it is worth exploring. When watching shorebirds on a mudflat or tidal inlet, a sudden panicked flight of your subjects often means a falcon is nearby, perhaps even flying low to the ground in hopes of surprising a lagging individual.

Even birds that are not being actively pursued can tip you off to a raptor nearby. If a bird stops and turns its head to glance to the sky, you should do the same. It's not uncommon for a raptor to be soaring high above, perhaps even beyond what you can see with the naked eye. When you're dinner, it pays to know where the diners are.

Tips to remember:

1. When identifying raptors, try to break them down into group first. Accipiters have long tails and relatively short wings. Buteos have long, broad wings and short tails. Falcons and kites have pointed wings. But any bird can change its look depending on the wind.

2. Large flocks of circling birds are called "kettles" and can contain a number of different species. Be sure to check them thoroughly.

3. Look for reactions of birds to find raptors flying high above.

Other Birds to Look for When You're Looking for Raptors: Conditions that are good for soaring raptors are often good for other soaring birds. It's not uncommon for hawk watchers to see good numbers of American White Pelicans, Sandhill Cranes, and Wood Storks (depending on your location), all of which use thermals of rising air to get around. Smaller aerial birds like swifts and swallows will also take advantage of a good flight day, and be sure to keep an eye on the trees and bushes around the platform for migratory passerines (perching birds) too.

FINDING SHOREBIRDS

We often think of shorebirds as background accessories to our beach vacation, but they're regular and readily seen across the continent. This is an incredibly diverse group, ranging from the omnipresent parking lot Killdeer to sandpipers that cross the ocean twice a year in migration. Like waterfowl, many shorebirds are highly migratory, breeding on the tundra of northern Canada and Alaska and wintering as far south as the southern tip of South America. For birders who want to see them, picking them up on migration is key.

While shorebirds can be seen in the spring, fall is generally the best time for really exploring this fascinating group of birds. Summer in the arctic is productive, but short, and most species have wrapped up raising chicks by July, at which point they have no reason to stick around. Adult shorebirds begin to arrive in the Lower 48 at the end of that month, leaving the chicks of the year to fend for themselves. From July till October, those first-year birds trickle southward, showing up on beaches, sod farms, mudflats, and water-treatment facilities across the continent. They make a lot of mistakes along the way, so for rare-bird aficionados, fall "shorebirding" season is prime time to look for those rare vagrants from Europe and Asia, most of which are recently fledged individuals.

While identification of some species of shorebirds can be tough, finding shorebirds isn't. Pretty much any shallow standing water will host some of the more common species, including nearly all of those dastardly "peeps" of the genus *Calidris*. A notoriously difficult group of birds for novice birders (and often for experienced birders too), many of these species are regulars at those muddy margins between water and land called mudflats.

Some shorebirds, like these Purple Sandpipers, prefer rugged rocky shorelines to sandy beaches.

Some birders break down other groups of shorebirds according to habitat preferences. So-called "grasspipers," like Buff-Breasted Sandpiper, Baird's Sandpiper, and others, like close-cut grass rather than mud. "Rockpipers," as you might expect, like rocky shorelines. This includes species like Wandering Tattler in the West and Purple Sandpiper in the East.

Depending on the species, you may have an entire season or a very narrow window of time to find them. Your field guide should let you know about the habitat preferences of your target species. Be prepared to be confused at first, but you may end up loving the challenge of this amazing family of birds.

Tips to remember:

1. Focus on behavior and feeding style to narrow down your options when looking at shorebirds.

2. Shorebird habitat is ephemeral, so a spot that is good one year may not be the next. Instead of thinking in terms of places to bird, think in terms of finding habitat—shallow, standing water—which could be anywhere.

3. Don't be afraid to say "I don't know." Shorebirds are hard and not all can be identified. Focus on some you can get comfortable with before throwing in the towel.

Other Birds to Look for When You're Looking for Shorebirds: Mudflats can attract a number of different birds, including terns, ducks, and rails. Make sure you're looking carefully through a flock of shorebirds to find all the birds hiding within.

Finding Gulls

Want to make a birder cringe? Call that big, web-footed thing loafing on the parking lot a "seagull." It won't take long before you realize that this common misnomer is incredibly limiting. Gulls aren't found just at the sea. They like lakes too, and rivers and parking lots and dumps. It doesn't take much effort to find them. Heck, if you've ever tried to eat lunch on a beach, you know that the gulls are more likely to find you!

A little bit of experience with gulls as a birder, and you'll quickly realize that most of the gulls around you are of two or three species, depending on where in the United States or Canada you are. Those birders who love gulls, though, live for finding that oddball among the common birds, that needle in the haystack, the piece of treasure in the garbage can.

In winter months, gulls will congregate together at large roosting sites, generally near water and food. These are great places to look for anything unusual among the flocks of regular species. While there are usually plenty of gulls around throughout the day, early morning and late evening are the best times to see the largest number of individual gulls. The more gulls you are able to get in front of you, the better your chances of finding a rare one.

During the day, most gulls will be out in search of food. They may scatter far and wide, but there are places where they'll congregate, and traditionally, the local landfill is one of the more productive places to find large groups of gulls during the day. A self-aware birder realizes how weird this sounds but, hey, you go where the birds are. When looking for unusual birds, focus on what is different from the majority of the group. Focus on color, particularly the back (mantle) and legs, and on size. These are things that will stand out regardless of how the gull is oriented, and they will often indicate a different species.

Gulls go where the food is, which can mean parking lots as often as beaches.

Because gulls take three to four years to reach adult plumage, the variety of looks young birds can have is something that takes a bit of time to familiarize yourself with. Close study of gulls is not for everyone, and birders shouldn't feel obligated to get deep into it if you prefer colorful, less-confusing, families of birds. But getting a grip on gulls can be rewarding, and even within a large group of seemingly drab-colored, dump-loving trash eaters, there are spectacular species, like the dramatic Sabine's Gull, the nearly mythical Ivory Gull, and easily one of the most sought-after species in North America, the mysterious Ross's Gull.

Tips to remember:

1. When looking at gulls, look at mantle color, leg color, and eye color. These three things will help you narrow down what you're looking at.

2. Gulls are variable and, at different ages, have different plumage. Structure and size don't change, though.

3. Uncertainty rules. No matter how good you get at gulls, you'll never be able to identify every one. Some are just too tough. Learn when to let go.

Other Birds to Look for When You're Looking for Gulls: Gulls like water, and birding near water is almost always productive. Mixed in with gull roosts you may find good varieties of terns—smaller, daintier gull relatives that forage with spectacular dives into the water.

FINDING OWLS

Owls are charismatic and iconic and often serve as the gateway to birding for many people. Their nocturnal habits make them mysterious, and they can be difficult to find despite the fact that they're really quite common across the continent. In North America, owls range in size from the massive Great Horned Owl, found continent-wide, to the miniscule Elf Owl of the desert Southwest. While strategies for finding individual species may differ, on the whole, owls can be tracked down by considering the following strategies.

Owls are famously active at night, but you can find them in their daytime roosts if you're lucky and know what to listen for. As with daytime hunting raptors like hawks and falcons, small birds are particularly attuned to the presence of owls, and if they manage to find one roosting during the day, they'll gang up in an attempt to drive it away or at least make it uncomfortable. This behavior is called "mobbing," and it can be a great way to find a roosting owl. Simply listen for the agitated calls of chickadees, titmice, gnatcatchers, and any other birds, follow them to the source, and look closely at any dense clump of branches or vines. Birds will mob predators besides owls—squirrels, snakes, or foxes—but owls are a popular focus of this type of behavior. It's important to look very closely, because owls are excellent at hiding. You may not see it, even if you're certain it's there, but there's no better opportunity than mobbing for finding these secretive birds.

In late winter, when owls are particularly active and calling, they can be very responsive to a tape or imitation of their vocalization. It's important to note that tape playing (called playback by birders) is not always appropriate. Fake calls do impact birds, though it's debatable precisely how much and how negatively. In any case, it's important to take a measured approach when using playback, and not to overwhelm your subject with

Crows and owls don't mix, and often one of the most reliable ways to find owls in the daytime is to follow the sound of crows making a ruckus.

high-decibel repetitive calls. Use the tape to get the desired response, bringing the bird closer to investigate, then turn it off. And always be sure to use the tape only during the period when birds are territorial and before they begin to nest, which is the best time for a response anyway. Playback use during nesting can cause birds stress and lead them to abandon their nest before the eggs hatch.

Tips to remember:

1. Owls breed early in the year, and they're easiest to find when they call. So late winter and early spring, when they're trying to find mates, is prime owling season.

2. Playback works, but don't overdo it.

3. When coming upon a potentially mobbed owl, be sure to very carefully check every branch. Even the biggest owls are incredibly good at disappearing.

Other Birds to Look for When You're Looking for Owls: Outside of migration, there's not a lot of bird activity happening at night, but in the summer, owls are joined in their after-dark routines by a strange group of birds called nightjars or goatsuckers. It's hard to describe a goatsucker to a non-birder, but imagine a sentient piece of tree bark with a huge mouth and you won't be far off. Nightjars like Whip-Poor-Wills, Poor-Wills, and Chuck-Will's-Widows have distinctive vocalizations, the rhythm of which gives many of the species their names. They're devilishly hard to get a look at, with plumage that looks like fallen leaves, but for many birders in rural areas, their calls are the sounds of a summer evening.

Finding Perching Birds

I'm tossing most of the rest of the families of small perching birds together here because the strategies for finding them are similar. For the purposes of this section, I'm not just referring to the passerines, officially the perching birds, but also species that can be found in similar places. These include woodpeckers and cuckoos, which while not closely related to the passerines, are behaviorally similar.

The entire back half of your field guide is devoted to these birds, and they're incredibly diverse, from aerial swallows to ground-scratching sparrows and all types in between. The vast majority of birds you see and hear in a given area, particularly inland, are perching birds. As with most groups, migration is the best time to see a wide variety of them, and this is the reason why spring and fall are such exciting times for birders. A large variety of passerines are neotropical migrants, in that they spend at least half of the year in Central and South America and return to North America in spring to breed. Most perching birds are migratory in some sense, even though the distances they travel may be short.

A few of the strategies mentioned earlier for finding specific groups of birds also work here. Playback can be an effective means of attracting certain perching birds, though the same considerations should be applied: Try to limit your usage, and never use playback when birds are actively nesting.

I also mentioned focusing on mobbing chickadees to find owls and raptors. Alternately, reproducing the vocalization of a small-bird-eating owl, like a screech or pygmy owl, either with playback or with your voice, can attract groups of passerines that will come in to investigate. This is particularly useful in the fall, as large numbers of newly fledged birds are more easily fooled by imitations than the experienced adults.

Listening for vocalizations is key. You don't have to be able to identify the bird by that chip note in the bushes, but hearing a bird sound will help you know where to look. In my own birding, 90 percent of the birds I find, I first locate because I hear something and then follow up on it.

When thinking about finding perching birds, think about their food. Fruiting trees and vines are great places to check in migration. On cold days, focus your search where the sun hits the trees. This is where insects will be active and will, like clockwork, attract the birds.

Tips to remember:

1. Keep your ears open. Always listen for the sounds of birds and follow those sounds.

2. Warmth equals bugs. Bugs equal birds. On cold days, head for the sun to find the active insect life, and thus the birds.

3. It's easiest to find birds at sunrise, because that's when birds are actively looking for food after the long night, but any time of day can be good. And any sort of interruption that prevents foraging is helpful: A rain shower will slow down feeding, but when it lets up, it can almost be like a second dawn.

4. Diversity of habitat means diversity of birds. The more different types of places you visit, the more different types of birds you'll see. Edge areas where two habitats intersect, like a pasture that abuts a forest, are usually best.

5. Look for unusual birds in flocks of common ones. When scanning a flock of similar species of birds, learn to blur out the common ones and look for anything different to follow up on. This may be that rare bird you're looking for!

Other Birds to Look for When You're Looking for Perching Birds: Well, since perching birds are pretty much everywhere, this can just about mean anything. That's as easy as it gets!

These tips are hardly everything to consider, but keeping some of these things in mind will help you see more species of birds.

ACTIVITY 10:
USE eBIRD TO FIND BIRDS NEAR YOU

I mentioned eBird in Chapter 7 as a great tool for birders to make their observations matter to the scientific community. But eBird is also a spectacular tool for birders looking to find specific birds near them. The suggestions above are very generalized, but you can use eBird to find good and very specific spots for shorebirds, passerines, raptors, and other birds near you. In the past, this sort of information was usually available only to birders who were ingrained in local birding communities, but it's amazing how technology has allowed these birding spots to become more widely known and available to all. It's a wonderful thing, in my opinion.

Tips for using eBird:

1. Go to eBird.org and click on the "Explore Data" tab at the top of the page.

2. You'll see a number of options here; the most useful will be "Explore a Region" or "Bar Charts." We'll take them both separately.

3. **Explore a Region:** This is an option for getting an idea of what is going on in your area right now. Simply by entering your state or county, you can get a comprehensive snapshot of what people are seeing and where they are seeing it. It's also a really great way to plan a trip, because you can find the best places to look for birds wherever you are going.

4. **Bar Charts:** Bar charts are graphs that show seasonal abundance for different bird species in an area—essentially what time of year is the best for finding a specific bird. By searching for your home county, you will get a list of species that have been recorded there, with a line of green bars for each week of the year. The thicker the bar, the more likely an encounter with a given bird will be. A narrow bar means a bird is less common.

5. As you scroll through the species, note that you can click on a button labeled "Maps." This is the magic piece of information. Upon clicking there, you will be taken to a map page with stickpins designating where certain birds have been seen. You can determine whether those birds have been seen recently by noting the colors. By choosing a common representative of each group, say, Broad-Winged Hawk, Pectoral Sandpiper, or Yellow-Rumped Warbler, your map will populate with spots that are probably very good for all hawks, shorebirds, or warblers respectively.

I cannot stress enough how useful this tool is. I use it all the time, not only when I travel, but when I want to find specific birds to see in my home county.

Give it a try! But be careful, because you can sink hours into eBird if you let yourself!

ACTIVITY 11:
LEARN HOW TO PISH

We've talked a little about how to go about seeking out birds, but it doesn't take much to make the birds come to you. And one of the best ways to do that is by "pishing."

You'll likely be introduced to pishing pretty early on in your birding experiences, because it's used often by field-trip leaders in an attempt to incite the curiosity—and often the ire—of small perching birds. We mentioned that small birds, particularly chickadees, titmice, and gnatcatchers, are very aware of potential threats, and will often raise a small ruckus when they find a roosting owl, hawk, snake, or any other predator, and that listening for this mob of bird calls is a good way to find these mixed flocks.

With pishing, you're trying to imitate the calls of these small birds, and make them curious enough to come in to check out the scene. Birders do this by saying *pssh, pssh, pssh* or some similar variation. Generally the idea is to imitate the cadence and pitch of these small birds, so be sure to listen and try to match them. The best pishers can build up a group of small birds from practically nothing at all in only a few minutes.

The following mnemonics can be used to imitate "ishable" birds. Simply read them out loud. They sound silly, but they really work! Chickadee—*Chicka-ch-ch-ch-ch-ch* (quickly). Titmouse—*PSS-PSS-pssh-pssh-pssh* (first part louder). Gnatcatcher—*psst-psst-psst* (softly and slowly). Wren—*ch-ch-ch-ch-ch-ch-ch* (as fast as you can).

Be careful not to overdo it in one spot, though. Birds can get habituated to human calls and get "pished out" so that they stop responding. This usually happens only in places that are heavily traveled by birders though. As you might expect, pishing works best in the fall because not only are birds more likely to be in mixed flocks, but the flocks are mostly young birds who are more easily fooled. Try it out in your own backyard!

Chapter 9

THE BIRDER'S YEAR

One of the really great things about being a birder is the opportunity to watch the seasons pass. Even if you live in a part of the world where snow never arrives and the leaves stay on the trees, the birds keep to a pretty strict calendar. By paying attention to their comings and goings, you may be surprised by how closely they keep to it.

This chapter will focus on birding strategies for each of the four seasons. Obviously, there will be some differences between strategies in the North of the continent and those in the South, but no matter where birds are located, they are looking for the same things everywhere in the world, so the strategies overlap more than you might expect.

Birds are pretty reliable year to year, and after a while, you begin to know what to look for when looking for birds. I'll include some popular and productive spots for birding during each of the seasons—productive because that's where the birds will likely congregate during those seasons, and popular because where the birds are, you'll likely find lots of birders too.

BIRDING IN SPRING

For most birders, spring is the most exciting time of the year. The weather gets nicer, the trees begin to leaf out, and most important for the birds we're looking for, the insects begin to get moving. Migrating birds that spend most of the year in the tropics return in huge numbers to take advantage of this rich seasonal food source, and birders love to put themselves in a position to see as many of these transients as they can in the short time they're around.

Unlike in winter, birds in spring are generally motivated by one thing. It might be crude to just say "sex," but the desire to breed and, more practically, the desire to get to the breeding places, drives everything about the season. And a birder who understands that sees a lot of spring birds.

Spring birds are singing birds. Males of local nesters will begin setting up territories in late February. By the time the rush of migrants comes through in late April, they are usually singing quite a bit as well. Recognizing bird songs or even just paying attention to bird vocalizations, whether or not you can identify birds by song, will help you find birds. Even species that do not nest in your area and are only passing through on their way north will often sing every morning.

Unlike in winter, when food and shelter are important, migrating birds in spring can show up just about anywhere. Because birds migrate at night, overnight weather conditions can have a huge impact on where they end up. A late-night storm system can arrest migration and force birds down in unusual places. Alternatively, a strong wind from the south will give them a tailwind that sends them halfway up the continent in one night.

The important thing to remember about spring is that it's quick. Late April and early May are the peak times across most of North America, when the neotropical migrants make their mad dash north. Sometimes it feels like it's all over in a few days, but the brief madness of the season is part of the reason birders love it so much.

Popular and productive places to look for birds in spring:

1. **Everywhere** – It sounds like a joke, but it's true. I've seen warblers in fast-food restaurant parking lots, shorebirds walking around on soccer fields, thrushes at my kid's school, hawks over the city. You can't really go wrong on a good spring morning. Birds start moving around just before sunrise and tend to slow up as the sun gets higher, usually around 10 o'clock. So while not essential, earlier is better. For a brief period in late April and early May, the birds are truly everywhere; all you need to do is open your eyes and your ears, and you'll find them.

2. **Migrant Hot Spots** – While just about anywhere is productive during the right time of year, there are some places on the continent that, by virtue of their geography, are traditionally phenomenal places to watch migrating birds up-close and personal. These are spots that birders from across the continent will travel to at a specific time of year just to put themselves in position for spectacular birding. You can think of these as pilgrimages for birders, places where migrants can practically wash over you.

Usually, these places are in close proximity to a large body of water, which can pose as a sort of speed bump for migratory birds. I've detailed a couple of these spots below.

3. **The Gulf Coast** (Texas, Louisiana, Alabama, Mississippi) — The Gulf of Mexico offers a significant hazard to birds migrating north. Birds tackle it one of three ways: They can fly around it, traveling up the east coast of Mexico and Texas; they can island-hop, traveling from northern South America up, hop-scotching the Caribbean islands up to Florida, or they can just fly over it.

1. Circum-gulf migrants travel by land around the Gulf of Mexico.
2. Trans-gulf mirgants take off from the Yucatan Peninsula and cross the Gulf in one go,
a trip that can take up to 18 hours of non-stop flying.

The problem with the first two routes is that they can take longer, and when getting to the breeding grounds fast to nail down a choice territory is your number-one aspiration, speed is critical. So many birds just jump right over the Gulf—an epic journey that means they're flying for more than twenty-four hours: no food, no sleep, no rest. It's one of the more incredible feats of animal endurance in the world, and these 2- to 3-ounce (55 to 85 g) songbirds do it every year.

As you might expect, they're really tired at the end of it. And the first piece of land they see is often the Gulf Coast between the Upper Texas Coast and Florida's panhandle. Oftentimes they'll come crashing into the trees on the coast completely exhausted, particularly if they run into a weather system that knocks them to the ground with challenging winds. Such a situation is called a "fallout," and it can mean hundreds of thousands of exhausted birds arriving all at once. Despite their place in birder lore (birders will talk about particularly good fallouts with reverence), these events are actually pretty rare. Even so, birders who come to spots like High Island, Texas, and Dauphin Island, Alabama, often see dozens to hundreds of birds arriving each day, and going about their business without a care for the very nearby people standing around watching them. It's one of the truly awe-inspiring spectacles in the birding world.

4. **Southern Shore of Lake Erie** (Ohio) – Like the Gulf of Mexico, the Great Lakes can also throw a little hiccup into a bird's migration schedule. Many times, they'll congregate on the southern shore of the lake, waiting for a south wind to help ferry them over the water. The shore of Lake Erie near Toledo, Ohio, is one such spot, and in the spring, birders come from all over to enjoy these birds as they wait in lakeside forests for those good winds, often at very close proximity to birders.

The situation is not as dramatic as on the Gulf Coast, but the birds are more consistently present here for several weeks into May. They're so reliable that a festival has sprung up celebrating these migratory birds, one of the more popular events on the birder's calendar.

5. **North Side of Lake Erie** (Ontario) – As you might expect, this is also an excellent place for observing migratory birds for precisely the reasons that make the Gulf Coast great. It's the first spot of land the birds see after crossing a large body of water.

While these specific spots are excellent for world-class, mind-blowing birding, birders not in Texas or Ohio might be pleased to know that they can see these sorts of phenomena just about anywhere, but on a smaller scale. Birds are hesitant to cross any body of water, because it exposes them to predators, and during migration, the southern side of any reservoir, bay or river of significant size will produce some productive birding along the waterfront.

BIRDING IN SUMMER

Summer is typically a down time for birders. It's a time when most species are busy with the job of raising another generation and, as you probably would expect, are trying their best to be invisible. It's remarkable how well many accomplish this, as even the most avid songsters turn down the dial so as not to bring attention to the brood nearby.

After their chicks fledge, most birds undergo a molt of some type, either replacing all of their feathers or just part of them. For some species, this adversely affects their ability to fly (ducks, in fact, go through a period when they're totally flightless), so their care to be unseen extends beyond the last chick to leave the nest. Even those species we do see are often ratty, with missing feathers, meaning that the characteristics we birders depend on are often difficult to see. For birds and birders alike, summer can be a rough time.

But there's still hope. Southward migration for some species, particularly shorebirds, begins as early as July. By August, adult shorebirds, having finished breeding for another year, are already heading south in droves. Many waders exhibit behavior called "post-breeding dispersal," in which they just take off to parts unknown, often turning up far outside their range. Focusing on shorebirds and wading birds is a big part of late-summer birding.

Popular and productive places to look for birds in the summer include:

1. **Mudflats** – Non-birders might think of "shorebirds" as the sort of thing you might see at, well, the shore. And you'd be mostly right, but sandpipers and plovers are just as common, in some places more common, in the center of the continent. These birds nest on the tundra north of the Arctic Circle, and when they've finished nesting, they bug out. This usually begins in July.

   But as they move south, they don't limit themselves to the shore, as the name suggests. They turn up anywhere where they can find water and food. This can mean the shallow arms of lakes and reservoirs, sod farms, even manicured sports fields. Most reservoirs in North America sprawl like sea creatures across the flood plains of dammed rivers, and the arms where the water is shallow—providing such places are accessible—are often great places to find shorebirds stopping on their way south in late summer. These places are often dependent on seasonal fluctuations in rainfall in many parts of the country, so such sites can be hit or miss from year to year. Keeping in touch with birders via your local or state Listserv can let you know where productive mudflats can be found.

Large, wading birds, like this Great Blue Heron, often disperse widely after breeding is over in the late summer.

2. **Lakes and Ponds** – I mentioned the mudflats, but the lakes themselves can be good, too. This is particularly true when you're looking for wading birds like herons and egrets, fish-eaters like cormorants, and some species of waterfowl. Most of these birds also exhibit post-breeding dispersal in the summer. The behavior is precisely what it sounds like. After the young are fledged, the birds take off hither and yon looking for food. While many of the wading birds are found at similar areas as the shorebirds you might be looking for this time of year, marshes, lakefronts, and small ponds without visible mud are worth checking too.

3. **Niche Habitats** – While migratory birds can show up anywhere, many species of birds have very particular requirements when it comes time to nest. Some, like the endangered Kirtland's Warbler and Black-Headed Vireo, are exceptionally rare in migration and only easy to find in their breeding grounds: young jack-pine forests of Michigan and Texas Hill Country scrub, respectively. Birds show remarkable fidelity to their home territories and can be easy to find at expected places. And really, the only time of year you can be absolutely certain to find them in a certain place is in the summer when they're breeding.

BIRDING IN THE FALL

Fall is usually my favorite time of the year because not only do the birds that headed north in the spring begin filtering back south, they take their time doing it. Because there's no sexual penalty for a leisurely migration in the fall, many birds will linger at sites this time of year. If spring migration sometimes feels as though it's over in a flash, fall makes you feel like you get your money's worth.

Along with the more leisurely pace, there are simply more birds in the fall. In addition to all the adults heading south, there are far more young birds making their first migration. Granted, many times these birds are not as colorful as their parents, but they more than make up for it with their abundance and their *naiveté*. Young birds are more prone to making mistakes, ending up in surprising places at surprising times. If you're interested in seeking out rarities, fall is the season for you. Young birds also tend to be less nervous around humans, allowing for better looks. And they're more inclined to fall for the various tricks birders employ in order to bring them close. Pishing (described in Activity 11), imitating an owl call, or playing a tape of a mobbing flock of birds are all far more likely to work on young birds than on their more savvy, world-weary parents.

In many ways, fall is simply a continuation of late summer. In fact, many birders consider the first movement of adult shorebirds in July to be the true start of the ornithological fall. They're not wrong, even if you prefer to abide by the astronomical version, but the good news is that, by the same coin, you could consider fall as continuing all the way to the end of waterfowl migration, which may not see birds in their winter homes till the end of December. Six months is a long season, and it means you're not likely to miss it.

Popular and productive places to watch birds in the fall include:

1. **Hawk Watches** – Mudflats and sod farms that are so good in summer continue to produce into fall, but one thing that practically defines birding in fall is the clear, fall afternoon at the hawk watch, when the migrating raptors are streaming past in huge numbers. Unlike most birds, raptors migrate during the day, the better to take advantage of warm air thermals rising off the land. Because hawks require rising air to get lift, the best flights are usually in the afternoon, so you don't need to feel like you have to rise at the break of dawn.

   Hawks also tend to use physical landforms to orient themselves, so mountain ranges and peninsulas are excellent places to watch them drift southward. Several sites across North America host annual hawk watches, some manned by seasonal field workers and others by volunteers. All are excellent and accessible places for novice birders to get a feel for birding culture, to meet some great people, and see one of the most incredible mass movements of organisms on the planet.

2. **Estuaries and Tidal Flats** – If you're lucky enough to live near the ocean, the birding is great pretty much year round. In fall, though, when shorebirds head south in numbers and pile up on estuarine shoals and exposed sand at low tide, the birding can be spectacular. In addition to the flocks of shorebirds, you'll also find the birds that see those flocks as an easy meal. Falcons like Peregrines and Merlins are often nearby and not hard to spot. When the whole flock of shorebirds picks up in a panic, you can be almost certain that a low-flying raptor is on the prowl.

3. **Fruiting Trees and Shrubs** – As in winter, food is a huge motivator for birds in the fall, perhaps second only to the need to keep moving slowly and inexorably southward. Trees that fruit in fall, like dogwoods, bayberry, myrtles, and viburnum almost always attract migrant birds. Not only birds like thrushes and tanagers, interested in the fruit, but also warblers and flycatchers, attracted to the bugs swarming around the rotting berries. Even seemingly unappealing plants like poison ivy fruit readily in the fall, and birds cannot resist.

4. **Around the Chickadees** – In fall, most perching birds travel in highly nomadic, mixed-species flocks. With no need to hold territories or worry about protecting food resources needed for hungry chicks, birds show no hesitation to take up with others of many species. And across most of the continent, the core of these mixed-species flocks is chickadees and titmice. In the southeast, it's Carolina Chickadees. Farther north, it'll be Black-Capped. In the Rockies, west to California, it'll be Mountain Chickadees. The species are different, but the behavior is the same.

Mixed flocks offer a number of advantages for the birds in them. With a multitude of foraging techniques and targets, the food needs of the birds rarely overlap. And more eyes are more effective at spotting both food sources and potential predators. Chickadees are mostly non-migratory, but other, highly migratory species take up with them because they're excellent watchmen, er, watchbirds. And many birds are effectively multilingual, in that they comprehend and respond to chickadee alarm calls. Hanging out with the residents gives them access to the chickadee's favored foraging locations and heightened awareness. So finding desirable migrants in fall is often as easy as looking for chickadees. Remember the adage, "For warblers in fall, go where chickadees call."

Birding in Winter

For birders, winter consists of the months of December, January, and February. In most parts of the continent, it's cold. In the north, there's generally snow and ice. The days are short, and many people put bird feeders outside their homes to supplement the food birds are seeking this time of year.

For birds, though, winter can generally be seen as the heart of the "non-breeding" season. Essentially, it's a time when they no longer need to worry about holding and defending territories, they only need to worry about surviving into the coming year. And that means one thing—food. Winter is a great time to find birds in large groups consisting of one and often more species. With no territories to defend, birds relax their inhibitions around one another, and work together to seek out fruiting trees or insect swarms. For the birder, going where such groups of birds find food is the name of the game.

Popular and productive places to look for birds in winter:

1. **Bodies of Water** – Be they manmade reservoirs, farm ponds, beaches, or even water-treatment facilities, water is always a good bet for finding birds in the winter. Birds we think of as "water" birds, like gulls, ducks, grebes, or herons, will seek out any open water. One can often find great concentrations of many species near open water, particularly if you live in an area where most water freezes up during the winter. In those places, an unfrozen area can be packed with birds seeking a safe place for food and shelter. Even in parts of the continent where frozen water is not an annual issue, open water can still provide a great opportunity to get close looks at birds in the winter.

Species like the Red-Throated Loon breed in the far north,
and they are usually only regularly seen by birders in winter when they migrate south.

2. **At the Ocean** – Inlets or marshes will often host birds either actively feeding or sitting around waiting for a favorable tide. On the open water, loons, grebes, and many species of sea ducks (duck species that prefer saltwater to fresh) are often not far off shore.

3. **Fallow Agricultural Fields** – Any place where agricultural fields retain some cover over the winter can offer good birding. Sparrows, Snow Buntings, or longspurs will frequent expanses of fallow farmland where spilled seed might still be present.

4. **Fruiting Trees** – Be sure to note where winter-fruiting berries like American holly, barberry, or beautyberry are growing, because these shrubs will often host nomadic flocks of birds in the winter months. The red berries are almost like a beacon for birds like American Robin or waxwings, and more rare species can occasionally be found in these flocks.

5. **Dense Thickets** – In addition to food, birds will also seek places to avoid bad weather, and dense, vine-ridden thickets offer good shelter from wind and predators. Seed-eating birds like sparrows and finches will tuck into such areas and become extremely difficult to see. When birding around fencerows and unkempt boundary areas, be sure to listen for bird vocalizations, because that can be a trick to finding some of these well-hidden flocks.

6. **Landfills** – Birding can take you to amazing natural places. It can also take you to the dump. It seems odd, but landfills in winter can be really productive, particularly if you are into the mystifying and edifying study of gulls. Gulls, you see, are not all created equal. Certain birders (some might describe them as masochistic) love nothing more than to parse out the grays, whites, and browns of a flock of gulls

in search of something unusual, because within flocks of the usual gulls—and depending on where you live on the continent, these can be any number of species—are often uncommon or even rare individuals. And gulls will eat anything, so the landfill can be a great place to look for them. Don't try this kind of birding in summer, though, unless you want to permanently destroy your sense of smell. The gulls probably won't be there anyway.

7. **Your Own Backyard** – Winter is also the time when backyard feeding stations are going to be most productive, and if you are willing to take on the burden and expense of managing one at your home, this is the time of year to do it. It's important to note that birds do not require supplemental food at backyard feeders to make it through the winter, but they'll definitely take advantage of it. Seeds, particularly black oil sunflower seeds, and suet are easy high-energy foods for birds that will provide them with extra calories when the weather gets particularly rough. Also, many interesting and unusual birds are first noted by birders in the winter when they visit feeders, particularly when the weather is about to get really bad.

As you can see, one of the great things about birding is that it offers opportunities for exploration year-round. There's always something to look for.

Chapter 10

WHY BIRDS? A REDUX

By now, I hope you're ready to proudly call yourself a birder. I hope this because when we say that the populations of many bird species have declined in recent years, we say that both as a cause for concern and a call to action. Birders are by definition people who care about birds, and we need a world in which more people care about birds.

How you go about birding is not a concern. The important thing is that you do *go* birding. I don't say that simply because I like birds and I think the world would be better place if we all had something to go outside and look at. I say it because a world with more birders in it is a world that prioritizes wild places and wild things. That's the world that I want to live in.

Birders are watchers and record-keepers. We are observers. We're also witnesses. It doesn't take much digging to see that there are any number of concerns facing wild places and wild things in the world today. It's no different for birds. In fact, the very reason birds are so fascinating to watch is that they are excellent indicators of the health of the world. They're found nearly everywhere, in nearly all habitats. They eat nearly every kind of food. They're readily visible to people, and we already have a considerable historical perspective on birds, because people have been watching them since we lived in caves. We've been keeping track of them only a slightly shorter amount of time, and they're currently being watched by hundreds of thousands, if not millions, of people just like you.

There may be some who prefer to keep birding free of politics and the political polarization that's arisen over the need to pay attention to the various environmental concerns facing the bird population. In the past, we could sort of keep the sport of birding removed from science and conservation issues, but if the past decade has taught us anything, it's that it's truly impossible to maintain that separation anymore. To love birds and birding is to be intimately involved in their welfare. There is no longer any place to hide from unpleasant truths about their future. In some ways, this is a troubling parting of the ways, from the previous carefree way we enjoyed birds. The frivolous

Birding is not only rewarding for the birder, but important for the birds too. More people out birding means more people who care about their welfare and conservation.

pursuit of birding was a way to escape the cruel realities of life. But in a more important way, birding is becoming the essential activity of a group of people whose hobby takes them to the front lines of any number of environmental catastrophes.

We are all witnesses. This is a sobering realization, but one that gives real purpose to our passion.

Birding is still fun, don't get me wrong. There is still a wonderful group of people out there who will freely share their homes, their birds, their knowledge. We are one tribe, we birders, driven by a love of all things feathered and a desire to see more of them. Whether that translates as a call to do your part for bird conservation or as a desire to see with your own eyes as much as you possibly can, it doesn't really matter. We're all in the same boat.

I am proud to call myself a birder and thankful every day that I'm able to be a part of the community.

I hope you'll join me.

BONUS:
GOING BEYOND
YOUR BACKYARD

Birding around your home is great, but you're not going to appreciate the true
magnitude of bird diversity on our continent unless you get out and explore a
little bit. The following list consists of fifty species that you're unlikely to find in
your yard or neighborhood (unless you have an amazing yard or neighborhood).
It's a grab bag of the uncommon, the unusual, and the difficult to find. In short,
many of these are birds that require a little bit of effort to seek out or to identify.
But if the heart of a birder beats in your chest, then you'll see spotting these birds
not as an impossibility, but as a challenge.

Every single one is out there for the taking. Get out and see them!

Unusual Species to Go Out and Find:

1. Common Loon – Loons are sleek fish-eating birds capable of traveling great distances underwater. Common Loons breed across the northern part of the continent, and winter across the South on the deeper reservoirs and along the shore. Be aware of their gray-and-white winter look and massive harpoon of a bill.

2. Horned Grebe – You might be tempted to call grebes ducks, but they're a different family of diving birds, with smaller pointy bills and longer necks. Like loons, they prefer deeper water where they're less likely to find competitors like ducks and cormorants. Horned Grebe is a regular species on lakes, reservoirs, large ponds, and shorelines.

3. American White Pelican – One of the largest flying birds in North America, the impressive white pelican often soars in large groups. They breed in large colonies on the northern Great Plains, and winter in shallow lakes and marshes on both coasts in flocks that makes their size all the more impressive.

4. Brandt's Cormorant – The Double-Crested Cormorant is common continent-wide, but it's not alone as a representative of these gregarious fish-eaters. Birders on the Pacific coast can find this species along the oceanfront, where it is easily identified by the large beige patch on its face.

5. American Bittern – Secretive and mysterious, the American Bittern is common across North America but infrequently seen. Few birds in the world are as well camouflaged in a marsh, and your best bet for seeing one is often to spook it by accidentally walking too close.

6. Reddish Egret – This species comes in two "morphs," one white and one dark. Both can be easily identified by their foraging behavior: a madcap race over the saltmarsh, running, spinning, and flapping, while chasing fish in shallow water.

7. Green Heron – One of our smallest herons, the Green Heron is common, but secretive, in marshes and ponds. It's one of the few birds known to use tools, dropping sticks and leaves into the water to attract the tiny fish it eats.

8. Gadwall – It can get a bad rap for being on the plain side in a family full of dramatic and iconic species, but when clearly seen, Gadwalls are striking birds with subtle grays, browns, and blacks with just a hint of iridescence. Plus their blocky square heads make them easy to identify even at a distance.

9. Eurasian Wigeon (vagrant) – One of the annually occurring vagrants on both coasts, the Eurasian Wigeon is often among the first "rare" birds a new birder comes across. It's the Eurasian version of our common American Wigeon, and is often seen in the same places. Just look for the red head among a flock of American Wigeons!

10. Ring-Necked Duck – For much of the continent, there's no better indication of a rapidly approaching winter than a flock of Ring-Necked Ducks at the local farm pond. It is the standard "diving duck," and knowing this species backward and forward will help you pick out those more unusual species.

11. Hooded Merganser – Mergansers are strange ducks, with long skinny bills that feature serrated edges almost like teeth, the better for grabbing fish that make up most of their diet. Males have an impressive crest that they display during their mid-winter mating displays.

12. California Condor (rare) – Formerly extinct in the wild, the last free-flying condors were captured in the 1980s as part of a desperate attempt to save them from extinction. Now, at least 200 individuals of this impressive species can be seen flying as they once did in California, Arizona, and Utah.

13. Bald Eagle – They may be common across North America, but there's something about seeing a Bald Eagle that gets people excited about birds. They're also one of the great conservation success stories, as restrictions on pesticides like DDT, which caused thinning of their egg shells, allowed this great raptor to once again return to the skies over lakes and rivers across the United States and Canada.

14. Cooper's Hawk – If your feeding station is attracting a lot of songbirds, it's probably attracting at least one Cooper's Hawk. A long tail and shorter wings make this bird maneuverable enough to snatch birds right out of the air.

15. Swainson's Hawk – We think of hawks primarily as rodent-eaters, but Swainson's Hawks eat mostly large flying insects. Primarily a bird of the Great Plains, they're highly migratory, traveling back and forth from the pampas of South America every year.

16. American Kestrel – Few birds of prey are as beloved as American Kestrels. These dainty little falcons are common in open areas where they hunt bugs and small mammals. Both sexes are colorful, but the rainbow-hued male is easily one of the most attractive raptors in the world.

17. California Quail – The classic quail with the jaunty topknot, California Quail is a regular in the West, even coming to feeders in large family groups in the suburban West. A similar species, Gambell's Quail, replaces the California Quail in the Southwest.

18. American Coot – Non-birders often mistake these swimming rails for ducks, but one look at their feet and you can tell something is different. Instead of webbed feet, coot have lobed feet, meaning each individual toe has what appear to be fleshy wings. It's bizarre and amazing, and all on a fairly common bird.

19. Virginia Rail (difficult) – Rails are known to be difficult. They're secretive, mostly nocturnal, and most are fairly small. Seeking them out can be like looking for a mouse in a marsh. Virginia Rails are fairly common, though, and you can usually find them by listening for their strange grunting call.

20. Whooping Crane (rare) – "Rare" can mean different things in different contexts in the birding world. Whooping Crane is one bird, though, that is legitimately rare, in that there are very few remaining. That doesn't mean they're hard to see in the right place, however. Most of the world's population overwinters at Aransas National Wildlife Refuge in Texas, and you can see this stunning bird there nearly every year.

21. American Golden-Plover – Plovers are remarkable birds, running around fields and mudflats like little wind-up toys, and few are as gorgeous as a breeding-plumed American Golden-Plover, with its golden speckled back and jet black underparts. You can find them regularly in pastures and sod farms on the Great Plains during migration, and elsewhere less commonly.

22. Bar-Tailed Godwit (vagrant) – This species is rare away from Alaska, though it occasionally strays elsewhere, but it's notable for having one of the most incredible migrations of any bird on Earth. Twice every year, Bar-tailed Godwits fly non-stop across the entire Pacific Ocean between breeding grounds in Alaska and wintering grounds in Australia and New Zealand, a journey of more than 7,000 miles each way. It's such an epic journey, that their digestive system actually shrinks to practically nothing to save weight.

23. Pectoral Sandpiper – One of the more common migratory shorebirds in North America, its journey is pretty impressive as well, though it's mostly over land. For birders across much of the continent, this is the "default" migratory sandpiper, and a great one to know well.

24. Wilson's Phalarope – Unlike most birds, where the male is the more colorful of the pair, phalaropes have it backward. The colorful female lays the eggs, but the more subdued male sits on them and raises the chicks. In late summer, these birds gather in huge concentrations on lakes in the West, foraging by swimming in circles to create a vortex that brings food to the surface.

25. Great Black-Backed Gull – Non-birders often write gulls off, but birders know that within those large flocks at dumps, beaches, and mall parking lots, there's quite a bit of diversity. The Great Black-Backed Gull of the Atlantic coast is the largest species of gull in the world, and it's a true brute. The jet-black backed adults are the kings of the beach, eating just about whatever they can fit into their mouths.

26. Sabine's Gull – Not all gulls are quite so rough, however, and the dainty Sabine's Gull, a high-arctic specialty, is perhaps the most elegant gull in North America, more like a tern than a gull. Its dainty yellow-tipped bill and flashy wing pattern make it stand out wherever it's seen. It winters uncommonly on the coasts, and migrates over the center of the continent, occasionally putting down on ponds and lakes in the interior in fall.

27. Caspian Tern – There are tern-like gulls, and there are gull-like terns, and Caspian Tern is the most gull-like of them all. This very large tern has a huge blood-red bill that stands out at a distance.

28. Eurasian Collared-Dove (introduced) – Of all the non-native species introduced on purpose or by accident in North America, Eurasian Collared-Dove is one that birders seem to accept the most. Perhaps it's the fact that they're less aggressive than other exotics, or perhaps people just like doves more than sparrows and starlings, but the rapid spread of this species across the Great Plains and the West continues, and birders seem more or less resigned to its presence around feedlots and agriculture.

29. Short-Eared Owl – Owls are much beloved regardless of species, and the unique Short-Eared Owl especially so. A species of open spaces, it floats over marshes and fields like a giant moth, snagging dozens of small rodents every night. It's not always an easy bird to find because of its nocturnal habits, but seeing one is an experience you'll never forget.

30. Eastern/Western Screech-Owl – Both species of screech owls on either side of the continent fill similar niches. They're small bird–predators, and when those birds find the owl's daytime roost, they'll often mob the owl mercilessly. Knowing their calls and habits can be an effective way to find foraging flocks of small passerines.

31. Chimney/Vaux's Swift – Like the owls, these two similar species bookend each side of the continent. Swifts look like flying cigars in the air, and they gather in huge roosts in the late summer as they prepare to migrate south. Often these roosts, in abandoned chimneys in urban areas, can attract hundreds of people who come to see the spectacle of clouds of swifts returning in the evenings.

32. Rufous Hummingbird – Primarily a bird of western North America, the Rufous Hummingbird increasingly over-winters near feeders in the eastern part of the continent. They're extremely hardy for such a tiny creature, breeding as far north as Alaska, and can survive periods of cold temperatures by inducing torpor overnight, which slows their heart rate and breathing to nearly nothing.

33. Ringed Kingfisher (range-restricted) – The wide-ranging Belted Kingfisher is an easy favorite among birders for its charisma, but imagine a kingfisher the size of a crow with a nearly foot-long (30.5 cm), dagger of a bill and you have the Ringed Kingfisher of south Texas. The species ranges into South America, but southern Texas is the one place you can see it in the United States. It's a highlight of any trip to that very birdy part of the country.

34. Lewis's Woodpecker – Woodpeckers are unique for many obvious reasons, and Lewis's Woodpecker is unique even among woodpeckers. For starters, it's highly migratory. That's because it often fly-catches flying insects, rather than solely seeking out tree-dwelling larvae like many of the others. Plus, it's pink and green, which is a color combination that is pretty unique among North American birds.

35. Eastern/Western Wood-Pewee – Flycatchers are often considered to be one of the more difficult bird groups in North America to identify. Most are not particularly colorful and can be identified most easily by vocalizations. Wood-pewees, those on either side of the continent, are a great place to start learning flycatchers. They're distinctive enough that the subtle aspects of bird identification aren't overwhelming, and they both have great, unique songs that are easy to pick out.

36. Scissor-Tailed Flycatcher – A bird of the southern Great Plains, and a regular early-fall vagrant across much of the continent, the Scissor-Tailed Flycatcher is among the most dramatic birds in North America. With a long forked tail and an attractive pink wash to its sides, this bird stands out like no other on the continent when you spot it on a fence row or power line.

37. Loggerhead Shrike – Shrikes are falcons stuck in a mocking-bird body. Their practice of capturing prey and impaling it on thorn bushes and barbed wire has saddled them with the name "butcherbird." Sadly though, it's a species that is declining across much of its range as the scrubby fields it prefers are plowed under for agriculture.

38. Gray Jay – A bird of the far north and high elevations, Gray Jays are often associated with fir trees and cold weather. They have little fear of humans and can be found around campgrounds where they've learned to associate humans with food.

39. American Pipit – Easily one of the least-known common species in North America, American Pipits are easy to miss as they walk through fallow fields, sod farms, and beaches. Their earth-tone plumage and bobbing walk is distinctive enough however. Once you've picked one of these out, you can be certain you've arrived as a birder.

40. Chestnut-Backed Chickadee – You can find one or two species of chickadees just about everywhere in North America doing just about the same thing regardless of the species. Perhaps the most attractive chickadee on the continent, though, is the beautiful Chestnut-Backed Chickadee of the Pacific Northwest. The combination of the natty black-and-white face and the chocolate brown body is surely a winner.

41. White-Breasted Nuthatch – This species is common, it's true, but it's important to note that what we call White-Breasted Nuthatch might actually be three distinct but very similar species. The populations of White-Breasted Nuthatches in the East, the Great Basin, and the Pacific coast are all subtly different in plumage and voice, which suggests that in the not-too-distant future, we might be talking about three types instead of just one. It's a reminder that it's important to keep track of what you see wherever you are, even if the species seems common.

42. Sedge Wren – Like rails, Sedge Wrens prefer dense thickets of marsh grass, which makes them much harder to get a look at than to hear. But if you do, you'll find that this subtly patterned bird is one of the most attractive wren species in the world, not just North America.

43. Northern Wheatear (vagrant) – Northern Wheatear is a fascinating bird, nesting in far northern Canada and Alaska, but choosing to overwinter in subtropical Africa rather than anywhere in North America. It goes to show that continental boundaries mean little to birds. Even so, the odd mixed-up migrant occasionally heads the other direction and ends up in North America. They're generally seen on the coasts, but are possible in open country just about anywhere.

44. Nashville Warbler – Of the more than thirty species of colorful warblers in North America, Nashville seems like an odd one to single out, but it's found on both sides of the continent, meaning that just about everyone would have a shot at finding this one. And more, it's a good-looking bird with a very distinctive under-tail pattern that, once recognized, can help you put similar patterns on similar species into context.

45. Cerulean Warbler (difficult) – There are few warblers as stunning as a male Cerulean Warbler. It helps that blue is a pretty unusual color on many North American birds, and when you see the glorious sky-blue back of this bird, you can't help but be hooked. Cerulean Warblers aren't as easy to find as they used to be though, because their core Appalachian breeding range has been hit hard by logging, acid rain, and especially, mountaintop-removal mining. Knowing about this bird will give you insight into the threats faced by many bird species in North America and beyond.

46. Western Tanager – The four regular species of tanagers in North America are all stunning birds, but the Western Tanager, by virtue of its fabulous red-to-yellow plumage is arguably the best. A fairly common species in the right habitat in the western half of the continent, it often shows up as a fall and winter vagrant in the East too.

47. Savannah Sparrow – Novice birders often get hung up on sparrows, and the thought of three-dozen variably streaky, often furtive birds can be overwhelming. But the Savannah Sparrow is a really good one to know. For starters, it's found continent-wide, so you're going to come across it at some point. Secondly, it looks similar to but slightly different from a number of birds. This may seem like a bad thing, but what it means is that you can compare lots of birds to Savannah Sparrows by focusing on how they're different. It's the platonic ideal of a sparrow, and that's a useful thing to know.

48. Painted Bunting – Maybe the most impossible-looking bird on the continent, the Painted Bunting is a patchwork of colors that almost seem too incredible to be real. But they are real, and Painted Buntings are actually fairly easy to find in the southern Great Plains. Their rambling, jangly song rings out from shrubby fields and rocky outcroppings from southern Missouri to Central America, where they seem more at home among parrots and gleaming hummingbirds.

49. Orchard Oriole – A smaller, brick-red version of the well-known Baltimore Oriole, Orchard Orioles are found in thickets and shrubby medians. When the light is poor, they look like slender blackbirds, but when the light shines on them, the brilliant rust really shows. One of the more spectacular common species in North America.

50. Evening Grosbeak – These massive finches from the far North are infrequent visitors to the South. But when they do come down, because of poor seed crops in boreal Canada, they lay waste to seed feeders and feeding stations, downing sunflower seeds in incredible quantities. Most people accept that, however, because the presence of Evening Grosbeaks is infrequent and exciting, and they're such flashy birds besides.

ACKNOWLEDGMENTS

This book is, in many ways, the culmination of many hours in the field and in discussion with many hundreds of birders, from world-class experts to rank beginners. They have all, in some way, contributed to how I think about birds and birding, and I thank them for that. Thanks to Mike Bergin and Corey Finger of 10,000 Birds, for allowing me a venue to write and a large audience to write to. Thanks, also, to Jeffrey Gordon and everybody at the American Birding Association for the many wonderful opportunities that have come from being involved in that fine organization. And of course, thanks to my parents, Greg and Martha, for indulging my interest in birds at a young age.

To my favorite field companions, Noah and Julia, and to my wife, Danielle, whose patience with this birding thing has been extraordinary; thank you for your continuing support.

Thanks to Will Kiester, Christine Fisher, Marissa Giambelluca, and Meg Baskis at Page Street Publishing for helping to make this a project I can really be proud of.

ABOUT THE AUTHOR

A birder since before he can remember, Nate Swick is the editor of The American Birding Association Blog, author of the *American Birding Association Field Guide to Birds of the Carolinas*, host of the ABA's American Birding Podcast and a leader for ABA events, as well as a regular contributor at the popular 10,000 Birds Blog. He's been the long-time coordinator for eBird in North Carolina, and he is a current member of the North Carolina Bird Records Committee. He is also an environmental educator and interpretive naturalist with a passion for the diversity of all living things. Nate lives in Greensboro, North Carolina, with his wife, Danielle, and two young children.

PHOTO CREDITS

INDEX